Turning Distress into Success

Building Wealth and Passive Income by Investing in Mortgage Notes

D1601437

Table of Contents

Introduction

- How Easy is Note Investing?

Dedication

This book is dedicated to my son Talib, who inspired me
to become the bank. And to all of my mentors and
accountability partners who have helped me
on this journey, and without
whom this would not
have been possible.

Thank you!

Introduction

As a then 8-year-old Talib hopped into the car as school got out, he couldn't help being drawn into his father's heated phone conversation. Dad wasn't happy. In fact; he was outright frustrated, and it showed. It wasn't the first time this scenario had played out on the ride home after school either. As father hung up to greet his son, and attempted to switch modes to a more cheery one Talib asks *"Dad, why don't you just become the bank?"*

It was 2008. The US, and the world was in crisis. Having learned some very brutal financial and investment lessons in the new money frenzy of the housing boom of the early 2000's, I had shifted to trying to help distressed homeowners keep the roofs over their heads with loan modifications. It wasn't easy. In fact; it was a maddening process. The banks were in shambles. Their balance and asset sheets were in disarray, they still didn't want to give up a penny, even if it was the only way for them to avoid further losses. Even when they were willing to help, their processes were such a disaster that it was hard to get any common sense modifications done. We did them. But it wasn't easy. And the banks weren't much help at all.

People were going through real hardships. CEOs of million dollar companies were working for minimum wage at fast food joints, and that's if they could get the job when competing against hundreds of others. They needed help. And if the country was going to make it, people needed meaningful home loan solutions. And they needed them fast. Yet the banks still had 'the Vegas concept' - even if they lost on some, the house would still win overall as they remained diversified.

So the only way to provide real, meaningful, and valuable help to individual homeowners and families was to become the bank. Not to be a mediator, middleman negotiating on their behalf. But to have to power to actually grant them a reprieve, and give them a chance to keep their homes. Talib got it. And in that "Eureka" moment on a cold afternoon in New Jersey, I got it too.

That doesn't mean that there weren't a few hurdles to overcome in the process. My family's finances had taken a pretty good beating in the crisis too. And it's a big leap going from being a broker or intermediary to being a 'bank'. But that's when National Note Group was really born.

In the following pages I detail that journey, and how you too can become the bank. How regular individuals can turn distress into success for themselves, and others. How to really make money work for you, enjoy a great income and wealth building in a sustainable way, while doing a lot of good every day.

If you aren't in the financial position you want to be, see a gap between your goals and where you are now, or simply want to protect what you have, and grow it, and aspire to adding more value and doing good for others, *this book is for you.*

Turning Distress Into Success

Chapter 1:
Mindset

I know some of you are eager to skip right to the how-to of what to invest in, and how to close the deal and put money in your pocket. But if there is one thing that is critical to success, and sustainable financial success, it is beginning with a rock solid foundation. Without that all the gains and wealth in the world will ultimately slip away through your fingers like sand. And it normally happens a lot faster than you think. That doesn't just mean having to downgrade your lifestyle. It can put an incredible strain on personal relationships and your health. It will rob you of your potential and ability to help others. It will also steal your joy. Money certainly isn't everything. But protecting your finances and ensuring sustainability goes hand in hand with protecting your health, relationships, and family. Isn't that worth spending a few moments reading about this?

This book is about elevating your current investment returns, building sizable and lasting wealth, and maximizing your life. But more than that; I wrote it so that you can enjoy the freedom and wealth I have found, the joy and rewards of helping others, and reach your full potential in all areas of your life. I trust it will inspire you, and that once you realize the results for yourself that you won't be able not to share them with others.

But to get and keep all of this absolutely requires developing and acquiring the right mindset. This is critical, and not preparing readers with a stable foundation would be completely irresponsible. If you just want a get rich quick scheme there are plenty of them out there created by those that want to take from you, not help you. This is for those that want to go bigger, and keep it longer.

If that interests you, then this book is definitely for *you*...

The Mindset of Success

In my experience there are five keys to the success mindset:

1. Success and Happiness is a Choice
2. Deciding Where You Want to Go
3. Understanding that New Outcomes Require New Actions
4. Choosing to Take Action
5. Contributing is Rewarding

Success and Happiness are a Choice

What makes us successful in life? Why do some of us become great parents who raised wonderful balanced children and others don't? Why do some become CEOs of major corporations and others can't seem to keep a job? What makes a big producer as opposed to a small one? What is really behind success in life?

Most of us know people who fit these descriptions. We know people who are very smart, good hearted, and who work hard, yet achieve very little. We see others who appear less than brilliant, and seem to face indomitable circumstances, and yet achieve great success.

Everything starts within you. You must develop a winning self-image. You must have purpose, set goals, and *most* importantly; **you must know your WHY**. In order to create extraordinary results, you *must* set higher expectations, and always play at 100%.

Most people don't have success in their life because they settle. They love the comfort zone, and have a conditioned mindset that's designed to keep them 'safe'. The saying goes that there are three kinds of people; those that make it happen, those that watch what happens, and those that sit there and wonder what it's like to be one of those that make it happen. You can only do what you know. So if you know a little, you will only do a little. Educate yourself on the investment. Most people don't get what they want, but because they don't know what they want. Even among those that do have dreams, most don't take the action to equip themselves with the knowledge, tools, or take action to make it happen.

Clarity = Power
Power = The ability to act

We crave the ability to work for ourselves, and not have to depend on anybody. Not to have to beg, or be held ransom by others. Having the right mindset will give you the right **"attitude."**

This is the most important word in any language in the world. People will react to you according to your attitude. And you generally attract what you are. In turn, your environment and the people you choose to associate with will determine your altitude. If you want to fly with the eagles, don't swim with the ducks. It is having the right mindset with a great attitude, and planting yourself in the right environment, that will bring success.

If you do this and expect great things to happen, they will. You get in life what you expect. Expectation drives the creative process. You get and become what you expect. You expect whatever you think about. So the question is; what are you thinking about?

It took me 36 years to really understand how this works. It took for me to hit rock bottom to become a warrior (one who conquers oneself). I searched high and low, read books, and began to put what I learned into practice daily by creating new habits. In my experience I can tell you that life is definitely what you choose. Every choice you make puts your life into motion one way or the other. So choose to become a warrior, choose to be extraordinary, chose to be free. The choice is yours to make.

Defining Where You Want to Go

To get where you want to go, you must have clarity about where you want to go, and why. Take as much time as you need, but don't skip this fundamental step. Otherwise you'll always be blown around by the wind, without a sail, oars, or a compass.

Get really clear about what you want. You can start in the blanks below. Or if you plan to share this book and pass it on use some paper or make the answers the background on your laptop so that you see it every day when you log on and off.

Ask yourself:

What do I really want out of life?

_____

What do I want to achieve?

_____

What do I want my legacy to be?

_____

How do I want people to remember me?

_____

What do I want to teach and empower my children with?

_____

What type of life and lifestyle do I want to have?

_____

How much money is it going to take to achieve this?

_____

What kind of extra time do I need to create to accomplish this?

_____

New Results Require New Actions

"If you keep doing what you've always done, you'll keep getting what you've always gotten."

If you want new, better, extraordinary results, you've got to take new, better, extraordinary actions.

If you want to make more money, while having more free time, without having to exponentially increase the number of hours you work, and the level of physical exertion you put in, you've got to take a different approach. I tried many things. But for me, that truly pivotal moment came in starting to invest in mortgage notes. I had made lots of money before. I had invested in real estate before by fixing and flipping houses, and operating rental properties. But becoming the bank, and investing in mortgage notes completely changed the game. It elevated my life, as well as my finances.

Taking Action

Kudos on already taking the first and most important step – embracing this book. You are already on the right track.

Clarity and knowledge certainly add strength. But they are not unleashed, and transformed into power until they are put into action. Think of a martial artist who competes in breaking concrete blocks. Training, eating right, size and muscle mass, and learning technique can really make a lot of difference in both competing in the ring, and in smashing through concrete blocks. But nothing is going to happen until that is channeled with force and speed in forward momentum. How many "could have been" people are there out there? "He could have been a great ball player." "He could have been a Nobel prize winner." "She could have been a NASA astronaut." There isn't much that is more tragic than wasted talent and potential.

So keep up your momentum, keep reading, keep taking action, snowball the results...

Contributing is Rewarding

In life and in business the more people you serve, the more success you will see. In business it is just a mechanical, common sense equation. The more people (X) you serve with your product (Y), the more revenues you get (Z). X times Y = Z.

If you want more Z, just increase the X factor.

The rewards of serving more people go well beyond the revenues, the monetary gains, and the things that money can buy. Serving and helping others can certainly be therapeutic, and can be some of the best impact and non-monetary rewards you can experience in your lifetime.

There are many ways each of us can contribute. It is even better when you can get paid to contribute and spend your time doing what you are passionate about. In fact, it is a privilege.

For me it has been about providing housing, and helping others improve their finances so that they can achieve their personal goals and unlock their potential. In my world to contribute is to receive. And in this sector we certainly need more professionals, CEOs, and investors that understand the importance of service before self. I remember when I first learned about this strategy. It is so powerful on so many levels. It helps the country, the economy, companies, individuals and families with housing, and empowers investors to achieve more of what they want in their lives and for their families. I thought "If I can just share my knowledge of everything I learn with everyone who would listen, that it would be the start of a new beginning." And not just a new stage in my life, but in hundreds and thousands of investors' and homeowners' lives. In many ways this would be a catalyst for innovating a new era in the real estate, mortgage, and banking industries. One which better serves all individuals and their families, and the nation overall.

So I made the choice to spend a whole year teaching for free. I started doing workshops, sharing information, and educating investors with all of the knowledge I would learn from real deals and experiences. I noticed that the more I would share, the faster the company would grow. And the differences it has made in individuals lives has been breathtaking. This has all grown way beyond the impact I could have had on my own. Desperate homeowners have been able to save their homes, jobs have been saved, and individual investors have been able to use this to rebound from the crisis and leap even further ahead. I started with a room of just 20 people. Today I can say I've shared, and continue to share my knowledge with thousands of investors trying to get into this space and experience the rewards. Teaching and adding value to others gives me my feeling of fulfillment. I love to educate others who have the right mindset, and who are eager to push themselves to new limits to generate wealth. And this book allows me to spread the information to even more people and empower them.

Chapter 2:

Make Money Work For You

With the exception of the mental and emotional rewards of helping others, virtually everything we need and want today requires money. In fact, if you tried to go volunteer with a charity you'd probably find that it costs thousands of dollars, even for a couple week stint, for the privilege of loaning your time, intelligence, and muscle to helping others. You don't have to like this fact. But it is a fact.

This is even true of time. Time is money today. Even gaining more free time requires money. You can choose to trim down to a four hour work week at any time. Or even retire. But it can get ugly quick if you don't have income and some financial reserves to provide for your basic needs, and those unexpected expenses.

Among your other goals, dreams, and aspirations may be education for kids, travel, a better home, new car, or even more basic items like the freedom to buy a venti sized coffee, or super-sized steak, or play a round of golf when you feel like it. It all takes money. And we all know that retiring is incredibly expensive. So expensive that the vast majority of people in this country will never be financially prepared to retire. At least not with a roof over their heads, the heat on all the way through the winter, food on the table, small gifts for the grandkids on birthdays, and being able to avoid comprehensive health care.

The problem we've all encountered is that the general public has been set up to expect to leave school and trade decades of their lives in exchange for hourly wages. And this still applies whether you are literally working by the hour, by the day, week, an annual salary, or are even launching a startup or run a small business.

There is nothing wrong with working. In fact, most will find they want something to work on after a couple years of retirement. But there is a huge difference between having to work to pay the bills and keep up, versus choosing to work on something because you can and want to. The difference is night and day. Unfortunately; no matter how much you earn when trading your time for money, it is rarely enough. Our society and economy has been designed so that it isn't enough. Consider that as of 2015 Fidelity reported the average 401k balance in the US hit a new record high of $91,800. Yet, those balances drop by nearly half a few years into retirement. While employers are up in arms about a potential $15 an hour minimum wage, Zillow reports the minimum hourly wage needed to afford a mediocre apartment in many US cities tops $40, $79, and in at least one case over $200 an hour.

The only way to break the cycle and hack income and wealth to a level that really delivers on your goals and dream life, and does so sustainably - is to make money work for you.

When money works for you, you get to hack time. How much you make is no longer tied to the number of hours you can work, or if you can work. This is investing. Invest and put your money to work. Let it work for you around the clock, on weekends and holidays, when you are sleeping, when you are spending quality time with your better half and kids, and when you are on vacation. And once the amount of regular income your investments pay you each month exceeds your monthly living expenses you are free. Financially independent.

Now I'll show you how I discovered my best investment ever, where you can find the money to invest, how to negotiate the best returns, how to enjoy stress free investment management, how to kick risk to the curb, and how to help others in the process...

Chapter 3:

From Tenant to Landlord to Lienlord

There are many investment options and ways to put your money to work for you. While I still invest in other things, I now prefer investing in mortgage notes. But when it comes to passive income cash flow, value, low risk, easy management, and building great wealth, this is it.

Real estate and housing costs are a great way to bring together the concept of making money work for you and how to choose excellent, proven investments which have largely been responsible for the most wealth building in recorded history. And we are all familiar with housing. Even if you've never owned a home you know how expensive it is to rent, and how valuable and beneficial having four walls and a roof of your own can be.

From Tenant to Homeowner

Even going from mom and dad's house or a college dorm to having your first apartment makes a big difference in life. It is energizing, inspiring, and empowering. And it's one of the first building blocks of our basic needs. You can do some decorating, optimize your space for an efficient lifestyle, start building a life, and maybe even a family. But the big jump is when you move from renter to homeowner.

Like trading your hours and life for an hourly wage, renting is unsustainable, and highly risky. You are always held ransom to what landlords demand when leases renew. And you are always paying a mortgage payment, or for someone to own and profit from the property. You get to choose whether you pay for someone else's investment or your own though.

Homeownership delivers a ton of benefits and rewards. Some are directly financial, others aren't. The nonfinancial include children doing better at school, peace of mind, and more. Owning a home has a lot of financial advantages. Eventually you'll be able to own that property free of any mortgage debt. It has many tax benefits and breaks. Life costs less as you don't have to constantly be moving. And appreciation helps owners stay ahead of inflation, and actually grow wealth in home equity. That's when money and investments start to work for you.

From Homeowner to Real Estate Investor

There is another huge leap in life and finances when individuals branch out and extend to investing in other real estate. This can take a variety of forms from fixing and flipping houses, to buying and managing rental properties, to purchasing income producing commercial real estate.

This is a significant advancement as the profits from these investments can be used to offset living expenses and build real wealth. This is in stark contrast to the home you live in. Your home equity may swell over time. But personal residence equity isn't counted in net worth. Because you will always need a home and a roof over your head. Other properties and investments can be traded and leveraged and sold for tangible and usable gains.

It is here that you'll begin to be able to really make money work for you, generate extra income and cash flow, and beef up your nest egg, capital for philanthropic causes, or legacy wealth.

Unfortunately this is as far as many get. And they get stuck here with the returns and limits that these investment strategies offer. Acquiring undervalued real estate, improving it, and reselling it for sizable profits, and owning cash flowing rentals can be great investments. There is a place for these investments in every individual's financial plan and investment portfolio. While real estate trends, styles, and values certainly change over time, it has been one of the most profitable investments for at least 2,500 years. Real estate was the foundation of the ancient Roman Republic. And even far before that, nomadic people and tribes certainly enhanced their own wealth and prosperity by controlling natural resources including water, shelter, food supplies, and then trade routes. It became crucial for survival. Then various forms of rent were developed which created enormously wealthy kingdoms (land-lords), and then individual investors. One of these was John D. Rockefeller, the first American billionaire, and a pioneer in philanthropy. A significant part of his success is directly tied to real estate and **banking**.

From Landlord to Lienlord

There is one more upgrade. One that few ever step into. And perhaps this is one of the reasons that there is such great disparity in wealth and incomes in America today. There are some that take and take. But that's not everyone. And it's certainly not true of all of the top 1% of organizations or wealthy individuals. In fact, our wealthiest are by far our biggest givers. They give more than most can ever dream about earning in a lifetime, never mind giving away. So how do they generate so much wealth, and control so much money?

They take the next step and graduate to become 'lienlords'.

While they may own real estate too, lienlords invest in debt. They make loans, hold loans, and trade loans and financing. They are effectively banks. Some are literally banks, others are funds and organizations, and well as individuals. The most common form of this we are all familiar with is mortgage loans.

The US government is one of the biggest landlords and lienlords in the world. Then you have private equity and hedge funds worth billions, and legendary investors like Warren Buffett who is a huge real estate and mortgage fan. Check out his recent moves and balance sheet for Berkshire Hathaway and you'll see major investments in Wells Fargo, Bank of America, and in mobile homes (Clayton Homes) and mobile home lending.

There are many superior advantages of being the lender. The management is more streamlined, the profits higher, the returns higher than most realize, the security concrete. And one of the beautiful things is that it doesn't matter if real estate values go up or down, or units aren't rented, or there is storm damage; they still get paid. And once you dig in you'll find they only use a limited amount of their own cash. Right now they are using yours to do this. And they are charging you for the privilege of making billions off of your money.

The Banks' M.O.

Banks, lenders, and funds thrive by borrowing money from individuals, businesses, and other credit lines, then loaning it out, or making investments in debt. They then give depositors a percentage of those investment and business gains back in interest on deposits. This is how they make their money. This is how they have become the most powerful entities in the world. This is their 'M.O.'.

Banks always have their (and your) money working. When You deposit and leave money in your checking account you are giving them investment capital which they use to make loans and profits. It's rare you'd see any share of that. Today you might get a tiny percentage of the profits made if you have a very good savings account, or hold a sizable, long term CD (Certificate of Deposit).

However, most of your 'gains' are normally wiped out and recouped by the big banks through service fees, penalties, junk fees, and when you apply for loans. You pay various borrowing and loan origination costs (in addition to higher interest rates), even if you are really just borrowing your own money back.

This is how the banks keep getting richer and richer. And why most individuals seem to keep getting poorer and poorer.

In many ways it is the ultimate 'no money down' real estate deal. And the banks play it around the clock 24/7, 365 days a year.

It's insanely profitable for banks. Especially when interest rates go up and they may be making north of 10% interest, and even more than 18% interest on some types of credit. In addition to application fees, points, and other costs. And if the borrower doesn't pay, the bank gets to step in and keep their pledged property. This means homes, businesses, cars, vacation properties, and more.

For those that feel bad for the banks that 'appeared' to take a hit in the past. Don't. Consider that all other fees aside; on a modest $350,000 home loan at just 7.5% interest, the bank gets back $881,010.28 over a 30 year term. That's an extra $531,010.28 in profit, on top of getting the capital back. And consider that most people refinance multiple times, and carry mortgage debt for longer than 30 years; the bank makes far more off each home loan client. Even if the bank repossessed a home and sold it for half of what it was worth, and had only collected half of the interest, in addition to the upfront fees; they are still way ahead of the game in profits.

According to the Board of Governors of the Federal Reserve System there were almost $13.5 trillion in mortgage loans in action in the United States as of June 2015[1]. And that's just one type of lending that banks engage in.

How I Was Inspired to Become the Bank

I'll admit that it took me quite a while to really get just how powerful being 'the bank' really is. So I get that going from homeowner to lienlord is a big jump for many of you too. And it's not just the realization that it is a profitable and safer way to invest for your future. Or even a necessary investment to survive and provide. Even knowing that this is how the 1%, the aspiring leaders like Warren Buffett make their money doesn't necessarily make it easier. For many it is just scary and confusing enough to take that first step to being a homeowner. Nevermind wholeheartedly embracing real estate investing. That is until you get the right perspective, and harness the right mindset.

Sometimes this requires making a few of our own mistakes. I just hope yours aren't as painful and devastating as mine. And there are many that have had it a lot worse. But now I'm definitely tuning into the wisdom of equally learning from others' mistakes, as well as their successes.

Like millions of others I jumped into the real estate investing boom of the early 2000s. The exuberance was contagious. Even those wise enough to anticipate the markets were going to dip didn't expect it to happen overnight, and so harshly. Money was flooding in and piling up at a fierce pace. And there seemed no imminent end in sight. For most of Generation X it just seemed that they were finally getting it, and doing things right. And that the universe was rewarding them for their hard work and super intelligence, and very handsomely. You could even get rich as a club server, or office building valet in those days. $100 bills were handed out as tips to everyone. It's when "making it rain" was really born. Hitting the bank to scoop several thousand dollars to blow for a mid-week night out was nothing to be surprised at. And most investors wouldn't bat an eye at losing $10,000 or more on a bad decision.

But that all changed. And really fast. Especially for those in hot east coast markets that got hit first. While the media often talks about a crisis in 2007 or 2008, that was years after it hit markets like Fort Lauderdale, FL which saw the market turn on them in 2005 and 2006.

Overnight that dream and new money frenzy turned into a nightmare. The cash just stopped flowing. Properties stopped moving. The news talked about property values dropping 10% or 20%. In reality neighboring homes were selling for more like 30% to 50% or their previous sales prices. If at all. That was bad news for those that had piled up car leases, loan payments, and credit card debt to the tune of tens of thousands of dollars per month. The fear and contractions caught on and spread just as fast as the excitement caught on in the first place. Suddenly you couldn't get a loan even if you were a director at a major financial institution, or even chairman of the Fed.

Investors like me were over-leveraged, over-exposed, and in trouble. Even many of those at the top of the game winded up in lines of hundreds applying for the most menial jobs. Those that were really determined and innovative, found ways to turn their lemons into lemonade. Often that still meant hitting rock bottom first.

My lemonade stand was loan modifications. People were in desperate need of help. Forget trying to keep the leases on fancy cars, club memberships, and keeping up with the Joneses. People were losing their homes in mass. You'd think it would have made sense for the banks to help in the process. After all; they had made a killing, had the public bail them out, and would be just fine if they helped homeowners hold on to their homes until things got a little better. In fact, the crisis could have been cut short long before it did if they had helped generously.

But no. They were still locked in the greed mindset. The mindset that they made all the rules. And could bully everyone, and break all the rules, with no meaningful consequences. And even when they were willing to make deals and grant workouts to minimize their own losses, the processes and systems were so inefficient that they were virtually impossible to navigate. And instead of trying to make it easier or invest in streamlining the process of granting short sales, and truly meaningful loan modifications, it seemed that these lenders just turned to underhanded tactics to foreclose on hurting borrowers faster by robo-signing and falsifying documents, or prosecuting Realtors and borrowers for 'short sale fraud'.

It was during these dark days of desperately trying to fight on behalf of borrowers, and save their homes, while trying to keep bread on the table, and a roof over my own family's head that I decided to become the bank.

It was crystal clear to my 8 year old on that afternoon after school. And it just made sense. If I was going to really help people. If I was really going to be able to help them keep their homes, and get back on track financially, and do it efficiently – I <u>had</u> to become the decision maker. I had to be able to grant them a break. Give them common sense solutions. And ones that would help, not harm them worse. And in a way that was easy. I had to become the bank and lien holder.

There were obvious challenges in making this leap. But I couldn't hide behind those excuses any longer. Someone had to step up. My eight year old Talib nominated me for the job. And when your kids hand you that torch and looks to you to be the one, you have just got to find a way. That's when I became the bank.

Since then National Note Group has blossomed beyond belief. And now instead of just providing for my family and helping a few others by being the bank, we help thousands of individuals and families, while empowering more individuals to participate in being the bank and being part of the solution.

From Distress to Success

Whether you are already doing very well financially in a

solid professional career, or need to boost your earnings now; it is critical to invest and put your money to work for you in order secure your financial future. That's obvious. It's money 101. It's survival 101.

Real estate is a great investment tool. And that remains true in spite of recent ups and downs. And perhaps specifically because of those fluctuations, taking the next step to becoming 'the bank' is a critical one that has a place in every successful individual and family's investment portfolio.

Direct investment in real estate, starting with your own home is a sound financial launchpad. Flipping distressed homes and managing rental properties still have their place. But those that want to do even more good, and enjoy greater wealth certainly ought to investigate being the bank, and investing in loans, notes, and debt.

Thankfully investing in loan notes like a bank has become safer and more profitable, if you do it right. Those with extensive experience and that have been around long enough certainly know what not to do, and what mistakes not to repeat. We know not to over-leverage, not to be blindly bullish on markets, that we need to stay diversified, and always operate efficiently. And now investors are equipped with more data and historical data than ever so that they can more accurately navigate and forecast market changes, and there is more real cash and equity in the US real estate and financial industry than there has been in decades.

So let's investigate how this type of investment works, how individuals can participate, and when the right time to apply this strategy is...

Turning Distress Into Success

Chapter 4:
The Power of the Paper

They say "He who holds the gold makes the rules." That means there is a lot of power in not just having the money to loan and invest, but in holding the paper.

In fact, a loan note can be worth far, far, more than just plain old cash or gold bullion.

An Introduction to Mortgage Loan Notes

There are many types of loans made by US banks and lenders. For now let's focus on the biggest dollar pool of loan notes out there – mortgage loans.

When a homebuyer or homeowner takes out a loan to purchase or refinance their property, a mortgage and promissory note are created. Note that this process and terminology can vary from state to state, and applies to commercial properties as well as residential ones. But the borrower receives the loan proceeds (money) in exchange for executing a promissory note (the promise to repay).

The borrower becomes the mortgagor, and gives the mortgagee a lien against their property as collateral. If the borrower fails to perform according to the note the lender may foreclosure and force the sale of the collateral or repossess it to satisfy the debt. The lien recorded against the property also ensures that the lender is paid off should the borrower sell the property, or seek to refinance.

In this process the promissory note becomes a highly valuable investment asset.

The noteholder is the one entitled to the interest, payments, and balance owed on the loan. These loan notes can then be held, sold, or traded as investments. And they are on a daily basis.

Lenders and banks only have so much money on deposit, and so much borrowing capacity at one time. And they mostly specialize in making loans rather than acting as servicers and collecting payments. They make money when they originate and make new loans. So they make loans, and then normally sell the bulk of them off. And then they repeat the process under their flagship brand names, as well as through various conduits and subsidiaries.

What few individuals, even real estate agents, mortgage brokers, regular investors, and sophisticated professionals realize is that these notes can be bought and invested in. It gets even better than just investing in, and replicating the best investments that the wealthy and banks participate in. It means letting banks do all of the hard work and heavy lifting upfront. And then tapping into that return stream. Let the banks market for customers, screen them, and do all of the due diligence on the property. Then acquire the streamlined investment as a note and reap the profits.

If you invest in these notes and acquire these notes you are then entitled to the remaining balance, interest, and payments due.

Banks and Mortgage Notes

Banks have been allowed to make the rules, control markets, and even operate outside the law with little more than the occasional slap on the wrist because they have, or at least control the flow of money. This could change dramatically over the next decade as more individuals realize they can be the bank, and get tired of being treated poorly by old institutions. But for now, banks, credit unions, and mortgage lending subsidiaries are still the main players in controlling housing and home loan lending.

Because they have the money that everyone needs they get to set the rules. They decide who gets the money, what they have to do in order to be able to borrow it, and how much they have to pay for the privilege of borrowing it. They even set the pace for repossessing homes and condos for those that slip up, or have trouble making payments. And this all enables them to control virtually the entire nation's real estate market, and the cost of living.

Old institutions lost a lot of this power after the crisis of the early 2000s as more individuals pulled money out of banks and decided to invest in alternate ways. And those that love conspiracy theories will have a field day in investigating how banks have profited so handsomely by orchestrating the crash, mass takeover of US real estate, and then cashing in on it in bulk through property sales and new mortgage loans. But that's a whole other book.

What you need to know is that banks have grown so big, rich, and powerful precisely because of their mortgage lending. They also get to choose who gets helped, and is

Fuquan Bilal

able to get ahead financially or not. Investing in mortgage notes and distressed properties has fueled the greedy. But it shouldn't just be about hoarding more money, and using families as puppets. Investing in mortgage notes, and being the bank is an incredible personal wealth building strategy. But it is also an opportunity to help other individuals, families, and the country to be empowered to be better secured financially, and enjoy fuller lives, with more opportunities. **If you can be a bank that cares about these things, while bolstering your own finances and life, then the country needs you to step up to the plate!** And you can't afford to sit on the sidelines and hope that one day those big old banks will change.

You Can Create and Invest in Mortgage Notes too

The beautiful thing is that all of this power doesn't have to be in the hands of a few unethical, uncaring, greedy corporations. This power, and these dynamics of the economy and wealth, can be democratized by individuals investing in notes too.

Regular individuals can create notes by financing homes and other assets and ventures. Or they can acquire these

37

wealth and cash flow producing assets after others create them. Although there is likely more regulation coming to this arena, there have been few if any barriers to most individuals enjoy the profits and rewards of these powerful investments. This biggest roadblock has been awareness of the possibility. Of course, as with any new investment, in order to invest safely, profitably, and efficiently it does take some learning. And to do it at scale, or truly passively it takes a new type of platform. That can take more time, investment, and large teams. And that's what we've built to make it easier for regular individuals with National Note Group.

So there are three main ways to invest in mortgage notes today:

1. Create your own
2. Buy and sell individual existing notes
3. Invest in a fund that buys and manages large pools of notes

Why Invest in Mortgage Notes?

What are the real, tangible benefits of investing in mortgage notes?

What are the practical advantages for you?

There are many including:

- Passive income and cash flow
- Strong returns
- Multiplying your capital
- Concrete security for your capital
- Providing real, and much needed help to homeowners
- Eliminating many of the challenges of old school real estate investing

These benefits are just the tip of the iceberg. The bottom line is that whether you are looking to beef up and supplement your current income, prepare for retirement, add lump sums of cash to your bank account to propel your portfolio, or just level up your long term wealth building - note investing can be a very smart move.

Note Investing 101

How basic note investing works in seven quick steps:

1. Know your why, and set your goals
2. Choose your note investing strategy
3. Determine which types of notes you want to invest in
4. Find out who has the notes you want, and can sell them
5. Perform your due diligence
6. Make offers
7. Collect cash flow, or execute on your exit strategy

Note Investing Always Works

One of the most critical questions that individuals should ask about any potential investment is, will it keep working?

Far too many individuals have found they have invested too much time, money, and energy exploring different types of investments or investment strategies and models, only to find out they no longer work. Or that their forward looking lifespan is very short. Few can afford that luxury. It's a huge and expensive trap. It applies to out of date real estate investing books and burning months in online forums where complete novices attempt to counterproductively lend their 'wisdom' and 'experience' to others. You'll be glad to know that this is not the case here!

Note investing always works. It works anywhere in America. And all the time.

Check out the constantly updated e-learning companion resource to this book at NNGNoteAcademy.com for more articles, videos, webinars, coaching calls, and live event announcements.

Note investing will always work because:

· There will always be a need for housing
· There is an ongoing need for development and redevelopment
· People will always need and benefit from lending and borrowing
· Home improvements will always need to be made
· There will always be a default rate

The longevity and need for financing is as strong as our most basic housing and food needs. It is never going away. There will always be a need for new loans to be made. And in order for loan originators to make new loans they'll have to sell many of the seasoned ones on to secondary investors.

To get a better perspective on just how big this opportunity and need is consider that according to a RealtyTrac report there were over $600 billion of residential loans originated in Q2 2013 alone. That was spread across 2.5 million home loans[1]. And during a period which many would still consider a slow economic period. Keep in mind that this is only residential home loan originations. It doesn't count commercial mortgages, business loans, auto loans, and other types of debt and borrowing. According to Nerdwallet, Federal Reserve survey data and U.S. Census data, as of June 2015 Americans were a total of $11.85 TRILLION in debt[2]. And again that is just individuals, not businesses. There were around $400 billion in commercial real estate loans made in 2014 according to the Mortgage Bankers Association[3]. And the CCIM Institute predicts there will be more than that invested in North America by foreign investors alone in 2015. While some expect foreign investment in US real estate to grow by 60%, by 2020.

Banks and investors are happy when these loans perform as they are supposed. But many crave the extra juicy profits and rewards of investing in non-performing loans. These will last too. **There will always be a default rate**. For one reason or another borrowers will default on loans, even in great economic times. They will go through divorce and separations, lose jobs, have health issues, businesses will flop, surprise expenses will come up, and people will miss payments. Even at the height of recent real estate and economic booms there were foreclosures. Not as many as in the global crisis. But they were there.

In the short to mid-term non-performing loans and notes (NPLs and NPNs), there are still masses coming online from the crisis that started in 2005. While many parts of the

USA saw their real estate markets earnestly begin to turn around as early as 2011, those that were hit last and hardest, we're still just seeing foreclosures blossoming in early 2015. Many of these home mortgage loans had defaulted years earlier. In other cases borrowers just couldn't hold out any longer. US banks and mortgage lenders had also been hampered in processing foreclosures and repossessing properties due to low distressed property values, court backlogs, creative borrowers, accounting rules and regulations, and in part due to their own widespread fraud including robo-signing and falsifying documents. For the most part, the flood gates have been opened, and new regulations and bank restrictions instituted in mid-2015 will force these note and REO holders to process these distressed assets more quickly going forward. This ought to facilitate even better discounts, profits, and ease of profits for note buyers and investors. Though there will be a more robust level of these discounted notes available to invest for several years. Especially when factoring in the mass re-default level on shoddy and unscrupulous bank loan modifications. Note that a report by the special inspector general for the Troubled Asset Relief Program (TARP), found that of HAMP loan modifications made in 2009, 53% had re-defaulted by 2015[4].

Note Investing Works Everywhere

Not only does note investing work all the time; it also works everywhere.

Note investing works throughout the United States. It works in every region and state. It works in every city, and neighborhood. It doesn't matter whether you are in a small rural town, or major metropolis, it just works. It works for commercial real estate, construction lending, home loans, mobile and manufactured homes, and even farmland. And at every end of the market, from micro-investing to prime property in Manhattan, San Francisco, and Washington DC.

Note investing even works overseas from London to third world countries (although the mechanics may differ depending on lending and land ownership laws). But it works. And yes, one day it may even work beyond our atmosphere. If we do end up vacationing on Mars, someone has to finance the billions it will cost to build those extreme intergalactic vacation homes and hotels.

And the vehicles to get there.

How Easy is Note Investing?

How easy is note investing really?

The truth is that note investing can be both incredibly easy, and unbelievably difficult. It really depends on the strategy, model, and path you pick to follow. And of course how much you invest in learning about it beforehand.

Investing through a fund type structure can make note investing incredibly simple. This is the streamlined approach to passive income. It's much like turnkey rental property investing, or a REIT, only with more safety, security, and less headache. This model means having a team of experts working on your behalf to source, negotiate, perform due diligence, and manage a note portfolio. You just have to sit back and check on the deposits being made to your bank account every now and again. It's truly passive income, with strong yield potential. But of course you still need to know who you are investing with, and have some idea of what they are doing so that you know if they are making smart moves.

Other investors may choose to get into hands-on note investing. This may be by buying properties and creating notes by offering owner financed mortgage loans, or by buying individual mortgage loan notes. This can obviously take a little more work, more education, requires constantly keeping on top of new laws and regulations, and stepping in to put out 'fires'. In some cases, for those that have the time and eagerness to learn, it can be more profitable. In other cases all the extra work and mistakes, and lack of volume activity won't yield net returns that are any better than the fund route.

Then there are those individuals that want to really jump into this in a big way. They can turn this into a big business venture. More volume can mean a bigger impact, and bigger returns. But there is a lot of work to be done to go from 0 to 60 when building a fund or note business. There is no one right choice when it comes to your level of involvement. The best path is the one which best fits your personal lifestyle and financial goals, and resources. And you can always transition as you go.

Keep reading and we'll show you the different types of note opportunities, how to trade like a pro, how to handle difficult borrower situations, how to minimize risk, tips for setting up your own note business, how to enjoy stress free success, and even where to find the money to up your note game if you are a little light.

Turning Distress Into Success

Chapter 5:

OPM

What if you don't have piles of cash laying around to invest in notes?

Not having enough money to invest is one of the most common reasons people give for not doing anything. Some have hundreds of thousands sitting on the sidelines or in poorly performing investments. Others might barely have enough in the bank to cover a couple months of expenses in case of an emergency. Some have more cash coming in than they know what to do with. Others are barely making ends meet. The beautiful thing is that when it comes to note investing, it doesn't really matter. This is not a brick wall that you can't scale.

Where do you find the money, and maximize what you already have? You probably have more than you think. Even if you don't; I'll show you how I've hacked the system, how to leverage new rules that help raise money, how to effectively and efficiently raise millions of dollars, and even become your own fund manager.

Turning Distress Into Success

This is a key section, whether you've got a million burning a hole in your pocket, or only picked this book off the floor in your friend's car as you were hunting for change for a soda.

Before I show you the money, let's crush a dozen other excuses people use to hold themselves back first...

Excuse	Solution
I don't know where to start	Finish reading this book
I don't have enough time	Invest so you can create more free time
Investing isn't for people like me	Everyone has to invest
I'm afraid to lose money	Invest fast, before your cash is devalued
I'm happy with the one investment I've got	Diversify your investments for safety
I'll just keep working forever	Invest so that you have a plan B
Wanting more money is just greedy	Know that note investing helps others too
The market might change	Create a portfolio that benefits from that
I can do it later	Realize how long you've procrastinated, and start
I'm just going to wait for a big inheritance	Be prepared for what you'll do with that money
I have too many expenses right now	Make money work to cover your expenses
I already have enough money	Protect what you have in secure assets

You Probably Have More Money Than You Think

Most people have access to more money than they think. Most of their cash and assets, and even liabilities aren't being optimized well. That keeps them working for money. And worse – working to support the investments and wealth of others. Those that don't really need more of it.

It is smart not to over stretch yourself. And having several months of emergency cash stashed for unplanned hurricanes, job losses, family medical emergencies, and even bailing kids, or parents out of jail is a smart thing. But too much idle cash is definitely a bad thing. And that's true whether it is literal cash in the mattress or a miserly bank savings account, an underperforming 401k, in your home, or in other depreciating assets. Remember that there are threats to all of these items all of the time. And even when they don't strike, inflation is fighting back and devaluing those assets and cash 24 hours a day, 365 days a year.

If you are fortunate enough to have all of the walls of your house packed with $100 bills, what happens when your house burns down or is blown away? That's probably not covered by your insurance.

Do you have extra cars that you aren't driving? They are either just collecting rust and going down in value, while costing you money, or they are costing you even more money in upkeep. The same goes for many other items.

Other individuals are frozen by the myth of owning their own homes 'free and clear'. Having a nice equity cushion in your home is a great thing. So is having enough money in various investments to pay off your home, or at least cover your holding costs in retirement. But the truth is that you never actually own your own home 'free and clear' in America. You are actually always paying rent. You might have a title deed. But you always have annual property taxes and other minor expenses. If you don't pay them, the government will foreclose and take your home back to rent to someone else. So in many cases it's best to have some level of mortgage financing, and to invest that money at higher returns. Then you can also take tax breaks. Many may also be able to refinance their homes and other properties at lower interest rates, and put the savings to use in investments. The same refinancing and restructuring principle applies to car loans, boat loans, private jets, and credit card debt.

Savings, and in particular retirement savings are an area where most aren't seeing their money work hard enough for them. Kaaren Hall, founder of uDirectIRA estimates that there are over $23 trillion in US retirement accounts. But, an Employee Benefit Research Institute survey in 2015 shows just 14% of Americans have $250,000 or more in total retirement savings[1]. JP Morgan's Retirement Savings Checkpoints says that a 35 year old earning $100,000 per year ought to already have a minimum of $140,000 saved. A 50 year old making $150,000 per year ought to have a minimum of $795,000 saved already. How far are you off from where you need and want to be? And these numbers are just about surviving. If you aren't there, chances are your retirement savings aren't working hard for you. One of the solutions for this is to take advantage of self-directed IRAs. Individuals and couples can establish in self-directed IRAs, or roll over existing retirements savings like IRAs and 401ks to self-directed plans. These plans allow investors to invest in a variety of investments including real estate and mortgage notes and other debt for superior returns, while retaining all the security of retirement savings accounts and tax free or tax deferred returns and growth. This can potentially help many to add double digits to their annual investment returns. Then compound those returns year over year without owing taxes on them.

Aligning Your Lifestyle with Your Grand Vision

Carrying on from the above, many individuals may just discover that finding the money to invest is simply about re-aligning their lifestyle with their grander vision for life and their goals and dreams.

This is crucial as we enter a new economic and real estate boom phase which creates new money, over-confidence, and propels the urge to spend. Hopefully most have learned well from their previous mistakes, and their parents' mistakes, and are better educated about finances and cycles. But those are lessons all too often easily and quickly forgotten.

Saving and investing needs to be the top priority. Investments should be made first each month, and out of each paycheck. Then those investments can pay for expenses and luxuries. Spending all you can, and then saving or investing what is left over won't leave much. And is virtually guaranteed to be a losing strategy. If your monthly bills and expenses are already choking you and your ability to invest, then they need to be dealt with. Slashing those that have a stranglehold on your wallet and family and time so that you can create a surplus should be at the very top of tomorrow's to-do list.

This may not be the fun part, but if expenses and debts already have the best of you, find a way to trim that spending. Invest and use initial returns to slash debt so that you can invest more. Then look at every dollar coming in, and ask what the best use of it is for achieving your ultimate goals. Fancy car leases, club memberships, and yet another pair of shoes that won't be worn, may better come from the proceeds of investing, and a reward for making those investments, rather than being used as a tool to get ahead.

Hacking the Money

This is where we start with OPM (Other People's Money). Even sophisticated investors with several million to put to work can benefit from leveraging what they have. The world's top individual investors like Warren Buffett and Donald Trump invest with other people's money as the new rule. And we've already seen how banks, mortgage lenders, and the largest hedge funds use other people's money to make more money. And it just makes sense. By multiplying what you have with leveraging you can reduce risk, enjoy more diversification and safety, and amp up returns. All at the same time. You've got to invest that money wisely and safely, with as much care as your own, if not more. But it can help you, and them too.

There are a number of ways to raise and pool funds. But before we dive into these, you've got to know your goals. And most importantly – **your why**. This is your compass.

Without your compass you are virtually guaranteed to end up at the wrong destination. And all it takes is to get off course by a couple of degrees and your destination can be thousands of miles away from where you wanted to go.

So why?

Why raise funds? Why invest? Why make more money? Not that we should condone any of his actions by any means; but even Al Pacino's character in the movie Scarface knew his why. Getting more money was just a means to an end. In this case it was to have more power and control over his life so that he could attract love and relationships. But he knew his why. Too many fans of the film, and perhaps the populace in general today get hung up on the money. Just getting more money for the sake of it. And few remember that money is very fluid. And unless you have a plan it will flow through your fingers like sand. It is either depreciating, or working for you.

*So ask...*How much money do I want to make? What will that money do for me, allow me to do?

Go back to your original answers in this book to remember what you want beyond money itself. How will it enable you to achieve those things in very specific ways? Use these questions and answers as your guide for all decisions. Once we recognize that every single thing we do and say, and every single dollar that we spend or give away, is either taking us closer or further away from our why, the sooner we can begin to operate fully optimized.

This will all help you live intentionally, and get on the faster track to your goals. You'll be able to pinpoint how much you need to earn in returns, and the investments you need to make to be able to achieve those returns and your goals. And you'll be able to more effectively raise the funds to multiply all of this.

Traditional Leverage & Fundraising Channels

There are many established channels for gaining more leverage to invest including:

- Credit cards
- Commercial real estate loans
- Business loans
- Personal and business lines of credit
- Unsecured loans
- Bank loans

While it is important to use credit wisely, it is one of the most powerful tools available to investors. Good, bad, ugly, overused, or underutilized, we all have credit. Again, this is one of those factors that is constantly either working for or against you. So make it work for you, wisely.

If you haven't already this may be the ideal time to start developing business credit. Build credit for an LLC or other legal entity which can leverage non-recourse loans, and separate your personal credit from everything else, while maximizing leverage capacity. Many will find that they can rapidly scale to wielding several million dollars very quickly.

Raising Funds from Friends & Family

One of the best and easiest sources of OPM is the friends and family you are already know. Those that already know, like, and trust you.

This can be a highly controversial source of funding for some. But it can be one of the best and most rewarding. Some people rush to reach out to friends and family, and everyone in their old rolodex every time the get excited about a new way to make a dollar. Others are afraid to let their closest contacts down, put their most valued relationships in jeopardy, or to put their ego on the line. Both of these mindsets can be equally harmful, to everyone.

The Pros of Funding from friends and family include:

· Efficient to raise
· Fast funding to put into play
· Zero hassle in qualifying
· Great terms
· A little patience and understanding when you need it
· Helping those you care about the most

Most of us have had that one 'friend' that has an incredible entrepreneurial spirit. They are filled with inspirational passion that overflows and bubbles over. Only they never stick with anything for long. Eventually, they only become your friend when they need early adopters or more cash. Yet, if you do really have something valuable that can help those you care about, you are really doing them a disservice but not turning them onto it.

Imagine one of your friends or siblings having the cure to a chronic medical condition you, your spouse, or children had, but they never told you about it. This definitely applies to finances. If you can help others not just achieve their nice-to-have dreams, but to provide the essentials for their family, secure needed health care and education for their kids, and give them the ability to provide for themselves through retirement and to spoil their grandkids, you must. You at least owe it to them to alert them to the opportunity. That's giving, not taking.

The best way to cross this bridge is often just to show them what it is doing it for you. If that's something they are interested in replicating for themselves, let them know how they can participate. If that means investing with you, or investing in you, that's not taking; that's helping them. Still, whether you go over this out at dinner, around your own kitchen table, or in your office make sure they are investing wisely too. Relationships are priceless. Great ones are rare and take work to develop, but can so easily be ruined. Maybe you'll begin by giving them a copy of this book to read, or help them get other parts of their mindset and finances aligned first. But at least for me; if I ever accept investment funds from people I know (or anyone for that matter) I tell them not to invest any more than they can afford to lose. *"While I am 99% confident in this investment, crazy and unexpected things can happen. So if giving me that much money to put to work for you is going to mean you don't speak to me again if i lose it – don't do it. Or start with a smaller amount."* Protect their interests, do everything you can to serve them.

The JOBS Act and Crowdfunding

The Jumpstart Our Business Startups (JOBS) act[2] came into play in 2012 and added a whole new dynamic to fundraising and investment capabilities.

Although the SEC is still clarifying and finalizing the finer points of the act and its various titles, the JOBS Act is empowering both organizers to raise funding from a broader cross-section of the crowd, and individuals to invest in a wider selection of investment opportunities. In some cases, such as in Florida, states have even paved the path and pre-empted further rulings by greenlighting expanded intrastate fundraising.

There has been a lot of buzz about the Security and Exchange Commission's ruling on Regulation A+, which goes into effect in the summer of 2015. Regulation A+ has opened up the door for firms to launch 'mini IPOs' up to $50M far easier than ever before. It also tears down old restrictions so that regular individuals can be told about investment opportunities and can invest in a wider variety of choices, even if they don't meet the old 'accredited investor' requirements.

It's really all about crowdfunding. Crowdfunding platforms have been gaining traction and evolving over the last few years. There are now well over a hundred crowdfunding website platforms ranging from donation crowdfunding via Go Fund Me, Kickstarter, and Indiegogo, to equity crowdfunding portals for startups, and specialized real estate crowdfunding options. These online platforms make it 'easy' for individuals and companies to raise money. So far it has been used to fundraise for everything from eating burritos to the Hard Rock Hotel in Palm Springs.

However, while the websites and names are new, the concept certainly isn't. Crowdfunding is essentially people getting together to fund things they care about, or which provide them a return for their investment. This has been done through various forms of partnerships, syndications, and groups for centuries. It's been used to develop and control real estate since at least medieval times by kings and queens, and on a very small scale by families helping each other buy homes to live in.

When it comes to investing in debt and notes, various type of crowdfunding can be used. This could theoretically include donation crowdfunding, establishing a niche crowdfunding portal, friends and family, partnerships, REITs, and participating in, or even creating your own fund.

Starting Your Own Fund

Starting your own legitimate fund can be a great option for those serious about operating at the top of the note and debt investment field. Call it a fund, hedge fund, or becoming 'the bank'; it's a lot better than being a bank cashier, loan officer, or solo private money lender. It provides the ability to accomplish a lot more, negotiate better discounts, and get access to inventory individuals simply cannot.

However, this is a totally different league than just investing in individual notes or properties; though there is nothing wrong with that. There is a right fit for everyone. But there is a substantial difference in operations, responsibility, and legal and accounting requirements. This is why most don't even have this option on their radar. It's why there are only a few thousand banks in the US, versus millions of real estate investors, and even more bank customers.

So if starting your own fund sounds like a fit for you, where do you even start? The second half of this book is mostly dedicated to how to execute on the mechanics of buying, selling, trading, and managing note investments. This is critical information for every debt and real estate investor.

And also essential for preparing to operate a sizable fund successfully. But it all starts with the setup.

Setting up a multi-million or multi-billion dollar fund also requires a superior level of attention. It is not just a matter of filing an LLC online yourself for $100, and then hitting the ground running. Even though the JOBS Act has brought down many barriers, new regulations like Dodd Frank are continuing to make lending a murky and more regulated industry. It is essential to be on the right side of the law from day one, and have systems to keep your activities, marketing, and accounting in check. Just a couple of paperwork mistakes can cost you a couple hundred thousand dollars, easily.

If you want to become a fund manager, and operate a fund, the first real step is to talk to a law firm that really specializes in this area. Securities attorneys and those that advertise help with organizing private placements are a good start. Saul Ewing is a large and popular firm in the northeast. They have offices throughout the major cities and business hubs of the region including Boston, New York, Washington, Wilmington, and Harrisburg[3]. However, it is important that new entrants to this landscape don't burn all their resources before getting started. Do always get the best legal and accounting help that you can afford. Don't throw away money. Wherever you are there are bound to be firms in this domain offering free workshops and free private consultations. You may even run into them at local real estate and finance networking events, and investor groups, or even happy hour. If these attorneys charge $400 to $500 an hour, every conversation you have for free piles up the savings. They'll help you drill into your action and to-do list, clarify costs, tell you what you can't do, what you need a license to do, and maybe even provide some great insight into what is working for others, and may even turn you onto money leads. Remember that you don't have to buy everything they are selling. Just get what you need. However, if you plan to raise millions of dollars expect professionals to charge a substantial percentage of that for top level assistance. That can run into six figures once you get going.

You'll also want to do the same with great accountants, bank managers, and others.

Raising Private Money to Become the Bank

No matter which of the above channels you take to raising money you'll need to get good at presenting, pitching, and closing. You need to be able to clearly present the opportunity that is available, your strengths, how it helps, and how you'll keep their money safe. This applies whether you are walking into a local bank for a loan, approaching a venture capitalist, or even trying to help your friends and family enrich their lives with smart investments. So where do you start? What materials do you need? How do you create more opportunities to raise money efficiently? How can you avoid self-sabotage by putting your foot in your own mouth?

The Warrior Pose

If you've ever practiced yoga you'll have seen the warrior pose. The warrior pose has several variations and advanced stages including the 'humble warrior'. While a great warrior pose may be a feat in itself, it's really used in the process of mastering one's self, and increasing strength, balance, and flexibility in order to achieve even more in other areas of life, as well as more complex and advanced yoga routines.

Before rushing out to pitch private investors, or raise funds, it is crucial to get your pose right. This is your stance, mindset, and the core of the body that will deliver. When raising private money you have to have the right stance, and be equipped to efficiently and effectively both raise money and deliver on the promises.

There is a clear and glaringly obvious difference between those that are trying yoga, or fundraising for the first time, versus those that have gotten some practice in. If you've ever tried yoga, you'll already know all too well the wobbling, muscle contorting sensations, and visible clumsiness that comes as a first timer. And you wouldn't pick an obvious first-timer as an expert yoga instructor would you? You want an instructor that looks and acts the part, and can help you get the same results. The same applies to investing, fundraising, and financial advisors.

So start by getting your stance right:

- Know your why
- Know how much you are going to raise, and by when
- Invest in your education, and have the knowledge you need

- Be supported by a great board of advisors and team members
- Develop great habits
- Create great branding and presentation materials
- Look the part
- Be confident

You attract what you are. Money comes easily and frequently when you have the right stance and expectations.

Make sure you can check off the items above and you'll find that *money is far more abundant than you ever imagined.* All too often the biggest challenge is that we simply don't set our expectations high enough. I remember when I started out raising private money and sharing these concepts and investment opportunities. We began with requiring a minimum investment of just $5,000. In hindsight; that was ridiculously low. It meant a lot more work raising money from more people, rather than raising larger amounts from fewer people. Now having other sophisticated and experienced investors and money managers call in eagerly wanting to invest six figures is just a daily occurrence that happens on autopilot. If you've invested in yourself, in your fund organization, and are achieving solid results you should be confident. Never undersell, undervalue yourself, and the value of your opportunity. That doesn't mean letting your ego swell to gargantuan proportions. Just understanding how much value you really have to offer. When I began sharing this information I was giving away at least $5,000 of information for just $200. No one bought it. Well, at least not the millions of individuals I hoped. When I made access to the information more scarce, optimized my time by taking note investing education online with webinars and videos, and raised the cost of training – students began flocking in! Even at $5,000 or $50,000 this knowledge and experience is cheap, but the point is that you have to not only make it easy for others to invest with you, but to maintain the perceived value.

Getting Organized

Beyond organizing and formalizing your fund or note investing business in terms of legal structure, accounting, and team members, the following are some of the specific items and tools that can be used in raising money...

·   Business plan
·   Credibility package
·   Prospectus or investment opportunity presentation
·   Pitch decks
·   Website

- Blog
- FAQs
- An 'elevator pitch'
- Social media pages
- Email marketing messages
- Business cards

Three Keys to Successfully Raising Capital:

1. Keep it Simple
2. Don't oversell
3. Pre-frame and win the capital before you pitch

Create good presentation materials, deliver them at the right time, in the right environment, never act desperate, be confident, and over deliver on your promises, and you'll never come up short of funds.

Pre-framing

Raising money isn't about hard selling on the phone Wolf of Wall Street style. Some might do it that way, but I wouldn't consider it to be the responsible or best way to go. If you are doing business right, and set up conversations well with good branding and deliver great results you shouldn't have to 'sell'. Their mind should be made up to do business with you, even before you have a serious conversation with prospective investors. The 'close' should just be a matter of them finding out how they can give you money to invest, signing any agreements, and wiring you the money. Good testimonials, visibility, and online branding materials can all help accomplish this with ease. Then even when you do make new contacts they can do their due diligence on you in seconds from their smartphones, on the spot.

Credibility & Presentation Packages

Follow up conversations and communications will probably involve sending credibility or presentation materials. These can take many forms such as pitch decks, printed prospectuses, or simply websites and emails.

They should look good, answer questions, and give confidence to readers. But they need to be simple. These are tools to facilitate, simplify, and streamline the process. They are to create action. If you make it too complicated, confusing, and just raise too many more questions you'll only be taking investors further away from investing with you, or stall them permanently. Be transparent, overcome objections in advance, use infographics, and include FAQs, but keep it simple, streamlined, and keep up the momentum.

Fuquan Bilal

Finding Private Investors

So who do you present these materials to? Beyond the above fundraising channels; crowdfunding, friends and family, and institutional lenders, how do you find more investors to connect with?

There are millions of private investors out there today. Some are full time angel investors. Others run family offices. Then there are simply regular individuals with cash they need to invest, and get better returns on. Some are already very wealthy, some are actively looking for opportunities like yours, others are average individuals that aren't aware of these options, but need a way to get ahead financially.

Seven ways to find more private investors:

1. Attending investment club meetings
2. Starting your own local investment club or meet up
3. Attending national events
4. Google Adwords
5. Blogging and other forms of content marketing
6. Social media marketing

7. Buying or renting lead lists

Nothing is really private today. We may not always love how much our lives are tracked by websites, and how often that information is shared. But it can be really handy when you want to find private investors. There are mountains of data out there. It can be filtered and overlaid to help laser target those that are a great fit for investment opportunities. Between credit bureau data, social media profiles, and Google alone there is enough data to identify individuals by how much they earn, how much they are worth, where they are, and the types of investments they like. You can even find out their favorite brands, bands, how much they owe on their mortgages, and where they bank. These lead lists can be bought, borrowed, and rented for direct mail, cold calling, internet, and email marketing.

For both these new contacts and existing ones, make sure you put all their contact information to use to follow up. Do so by email, phone, mail, social media, and in person. Organize this. Personalize it. Automate it! Optimize your time and conversion rates by automating emails, social media, direct mail, and other contacts so that once a contact is made they are followed up with until they invest and refer others. And don't stop there. Maintain contact with all of your regular investors, vendors, and strategic business partners. This can help generate a lot of repeat business and referrals.

Getting Help

Obviously from strategizing a fundraising campaign, to formalizing a business plan, to creating presentation materials, and marketing, there can be a lot of work involved. Some of you will have the time and expert skills to tackle these tasks by yourself. Most won't. It is time consuming and takes experience, but is vital.

Three options for finding help:

1. Hire an agency
2. Delegate to outsourced freelance experts
3. Recruit an in-house team

Today most of these marketing and fundraising tasks are often more effectively and efficiently handled by outsourced help. These on-demand services help eliminate overhead, maximize productivity and efficiency, and can keep up ROI. It is getting the best help you can, while getting the most out of your time, and every dollar. Check out outsourcing platforms like Upwork.com to find great freelancers to help out.

Note that much of this section also applies to liquidating investment properties, managing real estate and note investments, and the everyday running of a note investing business.

Chapter 6:
Exit Strategies

Note investing has many advantages, but one of its best perks is the wide variety of exit strategies and options available. No matter what your financial goals and aspirations are – there is a great exit strategy for you. So what are they? Which is the best option?

Start with the Exit in Mind

Successful investors and business people always start with their exit strategy. Never get in, until you know how you are going to get out. It is one of the most basic, yet most important of the investment principles. Know how you are going to make your money when you buy, and your success is far better ensured.

Your exit is when you have really recouped your capital invested, and your returns. Paper gains and losses in between don't mean a whole lot. The great appeal of notes for sophisticated investors is there many different exits. That means a great fit for a variety of timelines and investment strategies and goals. But perhaps more importantly; increased security. If your plan A doesn't pan out as well as you hoped, there is always a plan B and C which can easily be executed when it comes to note investing.

Let's look at seven potential exits for note investors...

1. Buy & Hold Notes for Passive Income

While buying and holding real estate related investments isn't normally seen as an exit strategy, notes are a little different. Over time investors get their capital and interest returned through regular installment payments. How long this will take depends on the amortization schedule and loan maturity date, or when borrowers decide to sell their property or refinance. So technically note investors don't have to do anything to exit their investments, except for collect regular checks or deposits.

2. Flipping Loan Notes & Note Brokering

Those looking for a faster exit, or desiring to generate larger lump sums of cash in the short term might finding flipping notes, or becoming a note broker is the right strategy. In theory this is a lot like flipping houses, only without all the extra risk, headaches, and work. This wholesaling approach is about buying low, and selling low to other investors that will implement other strategies. This can be done with individual loan notes, or in bulk with pools of notes. If you can source plenty of significantly discounted notes you'll find there are plenty of note buyers hungry for these assets and cash flow producing vehicles.

3. 'Rehabbing Notes'

Like rehabbing houses, investors can add value to discounted, distressed, and undervalued notes, and resell them for profit. The most obvious way to do this is to bring non-performing loan notes to performing again. This may be done via better borrower management which we'll get into a little later in this book. Or by loan modification. Bring the loan back to performing, increase its value with more appealing terms, and make them more attractive with seasoning. The notes can then be resold for more to other note investors.

4. Acquiring the Underlying Real Estate & Holding

While this may not technically be a complete exit it is a way to convert a paper investment to a brick and mortar one. In fact, many real estate investors have been trending towards using non-performing mortgage notes as a channel for acquiring discounted rental properties. It can offer deeper discounts and less competition. However, this can certainly be controversial. Acquiring distressed home loans with the intent of foreclosing on and displacing homeowners and their families when they are struggling may not be nice, if not of questionable ethics. Of course there are many properties which are abandoned, leasebacks, and commercial properties which may be a win-win for all sides. This is always an option to keep in your back pocket in case you need it, but more note sellers are trending towards selling their inventory to note buyers that want to help homeowners, not hurt them. In fact, 2015 saw major note pool auctions from institutions and government agencies giving preference to non-profits or putting restrictions on being able to resell properties within a certain timeframe. Sellers do, after all, have some responsibility in who they sell to. If not legally, at least in terms of morals, their brand reputations, and shareholder protections.

5. Acquiring and Reselling the Underlying Real Estate
In addition to foreclosing and renting out collateral properties for passive income, investors can also rehab and flip the real estate. This can often unlock huge profits.

Fuquan Bilal

This can be done on a wholesale basis, one-by-one, in bulk, with a little clean up, by rehabbing, or even tearing down and rebuilding properties. Again, it is important to watch your impact on individual borrowers, but there are certainly circumstances in which this can be a win for borrowers, lenders, note sellers, and the community.

6. Hybrid Exit Options
What makes note investing even greater is that there are not only multiple exit strategies, but there are hybrid options too. This way you can have the best of all worlds, and achieve multiple financial goals faster. Notes can be held for income, and then sold. Or a percentage of payments can be sold. You can sell some of the early payments for a lump sum check. This is perfect if you want to diversify into more notes now, build wealth, and can then retain a passive income stream for later in life when you may be retired. Or you could sell on a percentage of each installment payment and collect some income while reinvesting cash, or use it to pay for large life expenses like college tuition or a new car. Some can even use notes to acquire the underlying real estate, and then resell that property with a seller held mortgage, creating a new note for more money.

7. Sell Your Note Business

Those investors that organize themselves as a business can simultaneously build up its value. In some cases a good brand can see its corporate value far exceed its asset and note income value. A larger competitor or institution looking to enter the market, or increase their market share effectively may buy you out for your assets, income, talent, brand, or market share potential. Or there is even the option of going IPO.

Chapter 7:

Types of Notes

There are many types of notes to invest in, including many different types of real estate related loan notes.

Eleven types of notes to invest in:

1. 1st lien position residential mortgage loans
2. 2nd lien position residential mortgage loans
3. Home equity lines of credit
4. Construction loan notes
5. Commercial real estate loans
6. Business lines of credit
7. Farmland and agricultural property loans
8. Manufactured and mobile home loans
9. Secured personal loan debt
10. Auto loans
11. Student loans

Now let's take a look at how some of these types of notes are different for real estate investors, how they compare, and the advantages mortgage note investing can have over direct investment in brick and mortar real estate...

Why Mortgage Notes?

We've already talked a little bit about the power of the

paper, and note investing. But why focus on mortgage notes specifically?

Sometimes mortgage note investors buy mixed pools of notes which include some mortgage notes, and other types of debt too. This can often help to obtain the best discounts, and improve diversification. Other times, these note investors simply buy mortgage notes, individually, or in bulk. While all notes may have the potential to increase in value, and deliver truly passive income with high yields, mortgage notes are often seen as the safest investments.

Mortgage notes are collateralized by tangible brick and mortar real estate and land. Most of the value of these properties is normally in the land. That's an incredible type of collateral. It can't easily be stolen, driven away, or broken into. No matter what happens it will still be there. Most loans aren't made unless mortgage lenders determine that they would really be better off in the case of a default. So if a borrower stops performing, the profit and returns can be even higher for note investors.

It is also obvious that a home is the last thing that borrowers will stop paying on. When things get tough they will default on credit cards, personal loans, auto loans, and other types of obligations before they stop paying their mortgages.

Mortgage loans also typically involve higher balances, and longer loan terms. This makes them among the most efficient types of debt to invest in.

Residential vs. Commercial Mortgage Notes

What's the difference between residential and mortgage note investing? Residential mortgage loans are made on 1-4 unit homes that people will live in. Commercial mortgages are generally made on business property. This includes office buildings, multifamily apartment buildings, industrial and warehouse properties, mixed use properties, and retail malls. Sometimes commercial or business loans are made on residential homes, or they are made to builders or real estate investors. Most residential home loans are made based upon the credit and financial qualifications of the individual borrower, whereas commercial mortgages are more weighted to being approved based upon the value of the asset and the income potential of the property.

Commercial mortgage loans are generally far easier and faster for lenders and noteholders to foreclose on than residential home loans. But residential loans may perform better. Loan terms often differ, with commercial mortgage loans being larger and for shorter terms. Both can be highly profitable investments. It is really about finding the best fit for your individual portfolio, based upon your own timeline.

Some may also base their investment choice on helping others. With this in mind investing in small commercial property loans, and residential properties may enable investors to accomplish more in serving others.

1st vs. 2nd Mortgage Notes

Whether investors are more interested in commercial or residential real estate mortgage notes, there are still first and second mortgages to choose from. In fact, there can be third and fourth mortgages, although they are far more rare, in addition to lines of credit and home equity lines. Each has their own advantages and benefits.

The main difference between these notes is in their

superiority in lien status, and their returns. First mortgage liens are the first mortgage loans to be paid off in the event of a default or foreclosure. Then come second mortgages, and so on. For this reason first mortgages normally carry lower interest rates. Second mortgages generally carry notably high interest rates. Seconds are also often for shorter periods. For example; 10 or 20 years, versus the traditional 15 or 30 year loan term on first mortgages on residential property.

In a declining market, seconds, thirds, and lines of credit can be perceived as riskier. There may not be enough equity to fully pay off a second or subsequent mortgage in a forced foreclosure situation. Although, some states will empower lenders to obtain judgments against borrowers and collect anyway. In a stable and rising property market second mortgages can easily be one of the most profitable types of notes. Even in a downturn, discounts normally offset risk. In fact, whenever you decide to invest in notes, and whatever types of notes you choose to invest in discounts, and negotiation will determine the true risk, lack of it, and amount of potential reward.

Performing vs. Non-Performing Notes

Many of the same comparisons between first and second mortgage notes can be applied to the difference between performing and non-performing notes. Notes that are being paid on time, and that are in good standing are considered performing. Late and delinquent notes are non-performing notes or NPNs and NPLs.

NPNs can be further broken down to:

- 90 days plus late
- Non-accrual
- Charge offs

Different types of loans, states, and even changing laws over time determine how soon a Notice of Default can be filed, and how soon a lender or servicer can begin the foreclosure and collection process. Once delinquent loans reach a certain point lenders classify them on the books in a way that they no longer anticipate interest and income from them. Non-performing assets be slowly depreciate on the books to a point where they can be sold and a lower price can be justified. Once hope is lost of collecting our

Fuquan Bilal

recouping the debt and investment made, debt may be sold off to collectors or in the case of real estate backed loans, properties are sent to foreclosure. If a borrower signs over the deed in lieu of foreclosure, the property isn't sold, or if the lender is the highest bidder at auction, the property becomes real estate owned (REO).

Why on earth would an investor want to by a non-performing loan note versus a performing one?

1. Higher returns
2. Helping others
3. To acquire a specific piece of property

Obviously non-performing loan notes are sold, bought, and traded at far deeper discounts than performing ones. In many cases these notes can be brought back to performing, or settled in other profitable ways. Put simply; there is a greater reward in investing in non-performing notes.

This can be compared to buying real estate. House flippers intentionally look for the ugliest house on the block in order to renovate and add value to it, before selling it for a substantial profit.

Mortgage Notes vs. Brick and Mortar Real Estate

Throughout this book you'll find various nuggets on the perks of investing in mortgage notes versus investing in the bricks and mortar real estate, and why I, and many wise investors have made the leap to becoming lienlords instead of landlords.

Here are five more specific reasons investors choose notes:

1. Lower transactional costs
2. Ease of management
3. Reduced liability
4. We need good noteholders
5. Profitable regardless of the market

Investing directly in property can be a great move. It can be very profitable, impactful for others, and a smart part of a diversified, well-rounded investment portfolio. Yet, there are very specific advantages of notes, which can't be ignored. There are a ton of expenses exclusively involved in purchasing a home or commercial property. These include borrowing costs, and easily run into many thousands of dollars. Then there are substantial costs when it comes to sell too. Those are all dollars that could actually be invested in notes, and be earning you a return. Owning a property is riddled with liability too. In fact, it's a miracle more landlords don't end up in serious financial trouble. In today's highly litigious society rental property owners have to weather issues with contractors, crazy neighbors, malicious tenants, and much more. Then there is ease of management. Compare managing tenants and keeping a property up to code, and in top shape with simply collecting mortgage payments each month. There is a massive difference. A difference in personal liability, stress, ROI on time, and the amount of time freedom. Think about your investing goals. It doesn't matter much what the market does either, note investing always works. And for those that wonder about the longevity of notes, remember that all buildings have a finite lifespan too.

Owner Financed vs. Institutionally Originated Notes

There is another difference between notes. This is private

and institutionally originated notes. Institutional notes are those created when banks, mortgage lending companies, and other lenders extend credit and make loans. Private notes can be created by private individual lenders, and are often created when property sellers offer owner financing. Creating notes as a property seller can be a great move. It can reduce the tax burden when selling a property with a lot of equity, speed up a sale, increase the gross sales price, and convert the bricks into a more versatile asset and stream of passive income. Some small real estate investors will sell properties like this routinely with a goal of selling and cashing out the note. There are buyers for these notes like J.G. Wentworth and Peachtree. Most note buyers prefer the perceived safety of institutionally originated notes. They view these notes as having better quality, having gone through more due diligence, being less susceptible to fraud, and of course they are able to buy institutional notes in bulk.

So now that we've covered some of the many note investing options, how do you actually pinpoint the very best note deals, find notes for sale, and negotiate the best deals?

Chapter 8:
The Art of the Trade

In order to identify good note opportunities, optimize your time, and negotiate the most profitable note deals, investors first need to get a grip on what actually makes a note valuable, and what takes away from their value and appeal.

What Makes Notes Valuable?

20 factors that can impact the value and appeal of a note for investing:

1. Loan amount
2. Balance
3. Property value
4. Loan-to-value
5. Location
6. Market direction
7. Discount
8. Amount of remaining payments
9. Interest rate
10. Type of note and collateral
11. Term left on the note
12. Condition of underlying collateral
13. Other liens against the property or borrower
14. Borrower credit profile
15. Seasoning on the note

16. Maturity date
17. Performance of the note
18. Who is selling the note
19. Ease of acquisition
20. Occupancy Status

Determine Your Preferred Note Characteristics

We may not always be able to purchase our perfect note all the time. When buying notes in bulk you might get some ideal notes, as well as some others. But it is good to have a profile of your ideal note.

So what are you looking for? What types of notes fit your investment goals, timelines, desired lifestyle, strategy, and resources?

Perhaps you like the security of residential mortgage notes because it is what you are most familiar with, only have $150,000 to work with, and want at least a 10% annual return. This will help you start looking in the right direction, and make faster progress towards acquiring notes.

Begin your note profile here:

Targeted annual return: _____

Amount of years you are willing to invest your capital:

_____

Amount you have to invest now: _____
Preferred type of note: _____

Again, this may change each time you make an investment, or over time, but getting some clarity will definitely give you a compass, and help spur momentum.

Finding Mortgage Notes for Sale

So where do you begin with sourcing mortgage notes to invest in?

The good news is that there are a variety of places to hunt for notes for sale, including:

- Marketing direct to distressed borrowers
- Attending investor groups and clubs
- Real estate investors
- Note brokers and companies
- Banks
- Mortgage lenders
- Servicers
- Hedge funds
- Credit unions
- FDIC
- Private loan creators and holders
- Note websites
- National Note Group

The right source for you is really about your time and financial resources, negotiating power, and finding a reliable source. So how do we lasso those unicorns, make them offers they can't refuse, and then unlock the value and profit in great notes?

The Buyer's Package

Before you rush out to find notes that may be for sale, or start promoting yourself as a major note buyer to banks with distressed loans, it pays to have your Buyer's Credibility Package ready to roll. This is the equivalent of a home buyer's pre-qualification letter for residential property purchases. Obviously it is a little more robust when it comes to buying mortgage notes, or pools of notes. Sellers have been burned time and again by 'buyers' that haven't come through. No one has time and energy to waste going through that cycle again and again. Yet there is an even more significant reason for this. Who buys notes, what they do with them, and how well they manage them is increasingly a reflection and responsibility of the seller, and has the potential to impact the market as a whole. The fact that major sellers began ensuring nonprofits had a shot at loan auctions, and that limitations have been put on the speed at which some buyers can foreclosure on properties in 2015 attests to that. Note sellers, and in particular mortgage note sellers want to know that you not just qualify and have the capacity to buy what you say, but are also going to be able to handle what you by well, and are a responsible note buyer.

A credibility package should include:

- Your resume
- Financial statements/Proof of funds
- ID
- Proof of citizenship status
- Credit reports
- Articles of incorporation
- Certificate of good standing with the state of incorporation
- A copy of the operating agreement
- A summary of your last three trades

This all shows your liquidity, level of experience, relevance of experience, reputation, track record, and how serious you are. This information can be compiled in a variety of formats for different situations. You may want a printable version for in person meetings, as well as a digital version to email. The cleaner this package is, the smoother the process. Don't let it be a hindrance. Make it be a power tool that lands you the prime seat at the deal table.

Chasing Unicorns

Now equipped with your buyer's package you can get out

there and catch some unicorns. For note buyers 'unicorns' are those magical connections that connect them to a treasure trove of great deals. Unicorns are elusive. Everyone wants one. Unicorns don't like mingling with the riffraff. They never answer the phone.

So how do you land a unicorn, and get them to give up the goods?

These are the gatekeepers of the profit. They are bank and fund managers, special department heads, and they are always getting hit up by amateur buyers. Trying to get through to them by conventional mail, email, phone, and knocking on doors isn't going to get you far. Making connections and building relationships with these professionals is key to getting the good discounts and unlocking the best profits. Despite all the technology we have today this is still a people business. So whenever possible try to meet with these people in person. Once you make a solid connection, and prove your value as a reliable and easy to work with note buyer, they'll come back to you with great deals. These relationships can really be invaluable in finding the best discounts, notes, and profit margins. So where do they hang out? Are there hot restaurants in your local financial district where they may hang out at lunch or after hours? Are they spending the weekends at local yacht clubs and prestigious golf courses? Are there national conferences coming up where you can get a whole lot of unicorns in the tank at the same time? Yes, this can take money. But investing in going where they hang out can produce great payoffs. The other option is really digging into the internet, finding them on LinkedIn and Google+, and working the introductions until you can get their attention. Once you make contact, really invest in building that relationship. Don't be an annoying stalker or door to door salesperson. Find ways to add value.

Due Diligence

Just from what we've covered in this chapter alone it is obvious that there are a number of factors that can influence the value of notes, as well as a fair amount of due diligence hoops that investors have to go through to get deals. It is all worth it. But this also suggests that investors should be doing a fair amount of their own due diligence when sourcing and negotiating note deals too.

There are generally two phases of due diligence when shopping for notes. In phase one the seller will provide certain information. Note investors can conduct some preliminary due diligence themselves. But this can be limited based upon information received, and in order to stay efficient. You don't want to spend too much time and money too early unless you know you've got a deal.

In phase one you may get:

- Basic analytics on the pool of notes, performance, and borrowers
- Recent opinion of fair market value
- Occupancy status for real estate notes
- Bankruptcy status checks

In phase two, due diligence can include:

- More accurate independent opinions of value
- Credit reports of borrowers
- Title searches

Don't neglect your due diligence! Your findings can help in negotiations; ensure you are getting what you are signing up for, protect capital, and maximize returns.

Negotiating Note Acquisitions

This is where note investing really gets fun. If you love strategy, creative thinking, and the thrill of the deal this will never feel like work. It's exciting stuff. Equipped with the right information, taking the time to understand those on the other side of the table, and with your due diligence done you might be very pleasantly surprised at the big discounts and profits to be negotiated.

Finding distressed situations generally comes in hand with motivated sellers. This presents a better opportunity to negotiate larger discounts, and in turn uncover more value and profit. This doesn't mean taking a predatory approach or negatively taking advantage of the crisis others are in. You can still be a valuable, positive, solution. They need help, you've got it. You are there to help, and you can probably offer them valuable help, whereas others might not have equally good intentions.

You can check bank reporting for accounts of delinquent and non-performing loans using software such as

DistressedPro. Then there are also note sellers that actively advertise distressed notes on various note exchange sites.

However, just because you find notes and noteholders in distress doesn't always mean a streamlined, easy acquisition process. New investors can find this very confusing and frustrating. They begin to view sellers as crazy and difficult people, become bitter, and often quit. That's good for the rest of us. What this really comes down to is empathy and understanding the position of the seller.

Understanding your seller and their position is critical. As a part of your due diligence and pre-negotiation preparation you want to dig in and find out everything you can. There can be dynamics that outsiders just don't get yet. Banks are the perfect example of this. Just because a given bank may have millions in non-performing loans doesn't mean that they can sell them to you at the discount you desire in that moment. That remains true even if it appears on paper that it is in their best interest to do so. Why? Banks in particular are heavily regulated. They have to follow tons of accounting rules, they need to watch for asset to liability balances and requirements, and they have to keep shareholders from panicking. The individual decision makers that you deal with also have their own burdens. They want to keep their jobs. That means they can't make decisions that aren't good for the organization. They want to look good to their higher ups too. Sometimes their higher ups don't agree on giving away masses of assets for pennies on the dollar, even if it is really the best move. So investors can look for signs that a bank can and is interested in selling. This not only means the presence of distress and non-performing notes, but also recent note sales, the overall reported health of the institution, and more. In some cases an asset will have to be charged down or slowly devalued on the books over several quarters before a transaction can be closed. For example; a million-dollar note that may now be worth $250,000 to you. The banker might agree, but try explaining to your boss that you just gave away $750,000! If that asset can be devalued on the books over a year, the loss at the time of sale to you may appear negligible. You still get the same deal, but your banker contact doesn't end up in the unemployment line next week, and the bank's stock doesn't plummet to zero.

There are other scenarios in which noteholders aren't used

to selling notes in this way and have to be eased into it. Or they may need to sell a pool of mixed notes to make it work. For example; you might offer to take on a pool of mixed notes that include both secured and unsecured notes including second mortgages and credit cards or auto loans and lines of credit. This can help you score extremely deep discounts, and they get to justify the transaction.

This is also where your rapport building skills, and relationship building will really come to your aid and be an advantage. Note sellers and representatives will really help to make things work if they know you, like you, and trust you. Once you've proven to be a valuable solutions provider, you can expect further deals will go a lot smoother and faster, and they'll even bring you opportunities when they have notes to sell, or maybe will even refer others to you.

Negotiating notes in seven steps:

1. Make contacts and build relationships
2. Identify the ideal types of notes you'd like to acquire
3. Market and scan for note opportunities
4. Conduct due diligence, including on the individual decision maker

5. Open up negotiations
6. Hammer out a deal
7. Get it closed

Quick trading guidelines:

a. First mortgages trade off of a percentage of the current fair market value of the property
b. Second mortgages trade off of a percentage of the unpaid principal balance of the loan

JVs & Pre-Trades

The really big note discounts and returns are often found in much bigger and more diverse pools of notes. It can be pretty tough trying to go out there and snipe individual mortgage notes directly from banks. It's not impossible, and it may be far easier via other dedicated note sellers. But if you want to be in a wholesale position, and get rock bottom discounts as if you were the Costco or Walmart negotiator of notes, you've got to go big. The bigger the better. We're talking about millions of dollars and thousands of loans at once. This might stretch your monetary resources, operational capacity, and circle of competence. Joint ventures (JVs) and pre-trades are a great solution for this. Perhaps you have a contact that has $1M to invest and who is demanding the types of discounts you are getting. Or maybe you have become friends with someone else who specializes in unsecured notes. Why not partner up? You can take down a bigger pool of notes, at much deeper discounts, and everyone wins. Take down the pool together, then divide the notes up.

Quick Tips for Becoming a Better Negotiator

1. Keep yourself in optimal mental and physical condition
2. Arm yourself with as much information as possible
3. Negotiate with confidence, do not underestimate your value
4. Connect and trade tactics and strategies with others
5. Decide in advance what you can and can't do, leave room to negotiate
6. Don't be drawn into emotional negotiations, remain objective
7. Know when to push, and when to pull back
8. Always operate from a mindset of serving others
9. Read and sharpen your skills

If you haven't read Sun Tzu's Art of War lately grab yourself a copy. Other top negotiation books to fill your shelves with include Getting to Yes by Roger Fisher, How to Win Friends and Influence People by Dale Carnegie, Negotiation Genius by Deepak Malhotra, and Influence: The Psychology of Persuasion by Robert Cialdini.

Reselling Your Notes

What if you want to sell your notes? Perhaps you just want to get in as a note broker and flip some notes quickly for lump sums of cash. Others might just find they need more liquidity down the road, or there is a big life expense that arises.

If you've got a good and valuable note you should find no shortage of note buyers. But, before you sell off the valuable asset and income producing investment you've acquired or created consider that you may be able to sell a part of your note.

There are many partial note options, including:

- Selling a number of upcoming payments
- Selling a percentage of each payment

Who will buy my note?

- Other individual private investors
- Note brokers

- Mortgage companies
- Note specialists and debt investors

How to sell your notes:

- Contact professional note buyers online
- Call up your peers and see who is shopping for notes to buy
- Become part of a group of note investors and attend note conferences
- Set up a note marketplace and marketing campaigns
- Post on other loan exchange sites, ie. www.loanmls.com or www.fciexchange.com

If you simply Google "mortgage notes for sale" you'll find a few pages of options, including plenty of ads for companies and brokers looking to help you sell your notes. It is normally pretty easy to get in touch with the good ones. Find out their criteria and the price they will pay, which will vary over time with the market. The more buyers you get loans to, the more and higher offers you'll receive.

Those that want to get more aggressive in routinely selling notes, and to maximize their returns get proactive about marketing and promoting their notes.

Ten ways to market notes for sale:

1. Setup a note exchange site
2. Use Google Adwords for pay-per-click advertising
3. Join LinkedIn, use ads and join groups
4. Send direct mail to targeted investors
5. Email marketing
6. Join and attend local real estate investor and mortgage groups
7. Attend industry tradeshows and conferences
8. Market to local mortgage brokers
9. Cold call other note buyers
10. Advertise in industry magazines

Now let's talk about how to maximize your note opportunities efficiently...

Turning Distress Into Success

Chapter 9:
Administration

Greater success can be found in a greater process...

Optimize your process of investing and managing your note investing and you'll maximize your returns, and optimize your results. 'Admin' might not sound fun, but whether you are buying and flipping notes, or are acquiring a handful or notes over time, or are taking on a multi-million-dollar portfolio to hold onto for the long term you've got to have some type of organization, system, and process.

The scale and variety of management and tasks involved is really going to depend on how much you plan to invest or trade, and how active you really want to be. Maybe you plan to scale your investments steadily over time. What's important is that you take control of this now, and start as you mean to finish. So do you just want to pick up a few notes as a casual passive investor? Do you want to launch your own fund and be a multimillion dollar fund manager? Or do you want to become a note broker?

Avoid the DIY Trap

"Start as you mean to finish." It can't be repeated enough. Setting up the system and administrative process right now is absolutely key to facilitating your larger goals and the exit you want. Perhaps you don't mind being active in investing now, or maybe you want to build a legacy business for your kids. But one day you'll likely want to retire, take more time off for golf, travel, or lazing by the beach, or even to sell your business for a lot more. What you do now, will make all the difference later. It will make a massive difference in the value of your notes and your business.

If you plan to simply pick up a note or two to hold for a decade or two for passive income, that's one thing. As an investor you can simply pick up a note or two that meets your needs. Some note sellers will give you more data than you will need. This way you can't skip all the hunting and negotiating, and jump right to pre-screened opportunities.

However, if you are going to go any bigger than this you need your own system, process, and probably some help. If you try to do it all yourself you are really voiding the whole concept of making money work for you. If you try to do it all you are really just creating a new job for yourself. That can be a job with a lot more hours than you've had in the past. Don't just assume this position and hope that it will change later. That is unlikely to happen all by itself. If you will have an active role you need a real plan and a real timeline for stepping up to being an owner-investor. If that isn't immediately, what is that date?

Build a Team

Building a team is critical if you are going to do any serious amount of investing and business. Thankfully with a little creativity and using new tools and business practices having an excellent team doesn't have to be obscenely expensive, or cumbersome. In fact, following the best practices and tips here it will likely be far more affordable, effective, and efficient than most expect is possible.

First let's look at some of the core roles that need to be covered:

- Legal help
- Bookkeeping/Accounting
- General receptionist, organizational and assistant tasks

- Borrower management
- Marketing
- Due diligence
- Higher management and strategy

Depending on your strategy and how big you get you may also need to cover:

- Sourcing notes
- Negotiations
- Sales
- Fundraising
- Customer service
- Property management

All of these roles can be divided up between various types of help including:

- Vendors, merchants, and service providers
- Advisors, coaches, and mentors
- Strategic business partners
- Interns and volunteers
- Paid team members

Hacking a Power Team

There are several ways to 'hack' your way to building a power team for less. The first is maximizing the use of vendors and service providers. Negotiate the best deals you can with them and leverage all of the potential help and tasks that they can help with. Don't hire directly and pay more, and add to your management burden and labor costs when you can get it for free from an established pro. When it comes to notes, title companies are a great example of this. In addition to title searches, insurance, and closing coordination and notary services, title companies may be a great source of leads. They also normally have great attorneys on hand who can assist with a variety of tasks for free, or very close to it. This includes preparing contracts, tax advice, negotiating some factors, and more. Sometimes this can save thousands of dollars compared to going to your regular business or family attorney who may charge $300 to $500 an hour or more.

Every note investor and CEO should have a couple of advisors. Most new startups and solo investors can't afford or don't need an official board of advisors. But you can hand pick some very wise and experienced pros and leverage them. This could be having a cup of coffee with someone each week, getting a mastermind group together once a month for lunch or a round of golf, or simple email conversations. Again you can also attend lunch and learn sessions, webinars, and free strategy sessions to gain a lot of insight. Be mindful of their time, and try to add back as much value as you can.

Strategic partners can be a great part of the power team too. This can include attorneys, bankers, local real estate brokers, and others. Find ways to work together to refer business, collaborate on marketing, and leverage each other's resources. Maybe your attorney owns their office building and has a spare office suite. Perhaps you can use that space and their conference room while you begin to grow. You may even be able to leverage that space for free if you give them some title work. And they may refer you note leads.

For some tasks you will need and can benefit a lot from outside help. In-house staff can have its perks, but today everyone from the newest and youngest real estate startups to the largest multi-billion dollar companies like Trulia, Blackstone, and even the government are outsourcing in some way. Outsourcing means being able to leverage the very best minds and talent in the world, on-demand, at affordable rates. Using platforms like Upwork.com you can rapidly source, screen, hire, engage, and manage remote help. And Upwork even does a lot of your bookkeeping. That's all included in the freelancer's rates. You can use them for a one off project, a couple hours a week, or full time if you like. There are thousands of freelancers on Upwork covering everything from outside sales to online marketing, copywriting, graphic design, and more.

Smart Management Practices

Now that you can hire help from a whole world of workers with a click it is important to take a moment to ensure that you are setting yourself up for success when it comes to choosing who to bring on as part of the team, and how to manage them with maximum efficiency.

Smart hiring tips:

· Take time to define your needs and the role first, be clear in job descriptions
· Screen by feedback ratings and length of experience
· Choose quality help, you'll get more for your money
· Find those with industry experience so you don't have to spend time on training
· Learn to get out of your own way

Do not underestimate this last bullet point. If you hire great people and are clear about expectations you shouldn't have any problem in leaving them to it. Micro-managing is counterproductive and self-sabotaging. Hire great people, make sure you are on the same page, and are all headed in the right direction, while empowering them to do their best work. If you aren't an experienced manager and HR pro then consider recruiting a GM or project manager, and grow them into the position of running everything for you.

Chapter 10:
Borrower Management

There is one major challenge of investing in debt for those that are holding notes for income. This is repayment and borrower management.

In a perfect world loans are made, or notes are purchased, and borrowers just pay how they are supposed to and your capital and interest gets deposited in your account. The process is totally passive. But we don't live in a perfect world. And those specifically acquiring notes that are non-performing status will almost invariably have to tackle this at least once. So what type of borrower management is required? How can investors intelligently navigate this area to boost returns and serve others better? What if it doesn't work out as planned?

Acquiring Non-Performing Loan Notes

There are various stages of delinquency, especially when it comes to mortgage notes. This can range from a few days past due, to milestones such as 30+ days late, 90 days late, nonaccrual, in foreclosure, and if they aren't saved beforehand they can end up as REOs. Note that just because a borrower is late does not mean that this is a bad loan or investment, or that the borrower is bad, or beyond hope. In fact these can be the greatest opportunities to make a difference in helping others, unlocking value and superior returns, and revitalizing the community and wider economy.

So why do borrowers become late? Why do they get so far behind? What are the easiest and most valuable ways to work with non-performing borrowers?

Why Borrowers are in Default

There are numerous reasons that mortgage borrowers can be late on payments, including:

- Taking out bad loans they didn't understand and couldn't afford
- Rising interest rates and payments on ARMs, and other housing expenses like taxes
- Bank fraud
- Lender mistakes
- Poor money management
- Emergencies; natural disasters, death in family, job loss, or health issues
- The overall economy

As you can see; there is a very wide variety of circumstances that can cause borrowers to be late or fall into default. Many of them have nothing to do with the individual borrower simply choosing not to pay, or really just being irresponsible. This is truer and truer as we see less loan notes coming from the highly speculative subprime days leading up to 2005.

But why do they get so far behind? Being a borrower hasn't been an easy thing over the last couple of decades. Various forms of lender fraud and poor practices have aimed at preying on borrowers. From questionable loans, to forced placed insurance, not releasing insurance proceeds, and robo-signing, as well as mistakes with property taxes and title, many good and performing borrowers have found themselves in default and even in foreclosure. Often this had nothing to do with their ability or intention to pay according to what they agreed.

Once late, back interest, late fees, and attorney fees can add up fast, making it virtually impossible for many to catch up, even in good times. Then the entire loan balance can be accelerated and demanded all at once. What would you, or could you do if a hurricane blew your roof off, your lender refused to counter-sign the insurance check, forced placed new insurance on you, and didn't credit your account with mortgage payments? Then you are considered past due, thousands are added to your payment, and the bank demands the whole balance at once. What can you do? Not much. You've got an urgent leak, your bank won't talk sense, and really appears to be trying to steal your home. This wasn't an unusual scenario for thousands of homeowners around 2004 to 2006.

Then add to this the fact that lenders wouldn't speak to clients, couldn't do it nicely or effectively when they tried, and the government and lenders blew millions on warning hard hit homeowners not to seek outside help.

Check out this data on foreclosures from Statistic Brain[i]:

Year	Foreclosures
2013	1,369,405
2012	2,300,000
2011	3,920,418
2010	3,843,548
2009	3,457,643
2008	3,019,482
2007	2,203,295
2006	1,215,304
2005	801,563

Now consider that there may only be around 75 million homes in the US that are normally occupied year round. Add to this that RealtyTrac[ii] reports that there were more than 100,000 foreclosure filings each month from August 2014 to June 2015, and that foreclosure auctions and bank repossessions were still heading up as of June 2015. Bank repos were up $35.8% year over year. In parts of Florida in June 2015 as many as 1 in every 169 housing units received a foreclosure notice. Then there are billions of dollars in delinquent loans which banks haven't started foreclosing on yet.

This really shows how many were impacted by foreclosure. And this is just the tip of the iceberg of how many fell late on payments during this time. So they are not all bad, irresponsible people, with no intention of paying on time. There was widespread hardship. The question is how do note investors help those that are not yet back on track?

Creating Win-Win Solutions

Done right, non-performing note investing is all about creating wins. Wins for everyone involved. The old lender wins when they get to shed non-performing assets. The new noteholder wins when they are able to make that loan perform for them. The borrower wins when they can find an effective resolution. And the greater community wins when homes aren't left abandoned to rot, and when the economy is made stronger. However, this really all comes down the new noteholder creating a win-win between them and the borrower. So how do you do that?

Creating a solution in seven steps:

1. Get in touch with the borrower
2. Get a handle on the current situation in depth
3. Get to the root cause and dynamics involved
4. Find a personalized solution, or options that work in this individual situation
5. Make the process easy and more pleasurable than the pain they were experiencing
6. Get it on paper
7. Stick to your end of the deal

The economy has come a long way from where it was. The pit of the individual crisis has passed for many borrowers. It is about a fresh start. Yet, borrowers can't or don't feel they can talk to their lenders. Or they have been filled with too much fear, or too much false optimism. They often incorrectly believe that help is going to fall out of the sky from the government, that they can find some shady hack to live for free forever, or that it really doesn't matter what they do, and that the process or trying to get help is just too painful. The last part may be accurate when trying to deal with some lenders and servicers. But it doesn't have to be that way. The trading of the note is the perfect opportunity for a fresh start, new connection, and a brighter future. But it will certainly take both sides to create a sustainable win-win.

Sometimes this is pretty easy. In other cases it can take some work. But if you are really interested in making it work, helping others, and are operating in top form, you can do it. And for those note buyers that aren't really interested in this there are ways to make money from notes. But for me personally this is absolutely the best part of the business. It delivers some of the best rewards, and absolutely helps make a monumental difference in people's lives, and their family's life.

The first part is really getting in touch and connecting with that borrower. Let them know you are there to help and create a win for them. But you need their help to do it. You need to understand their situation and what they'd like to do if that option is available. Offer a graceful exit, or a sustainable and viable way to stay in place.

If they are ready just to leave and call it quits, then perhaps this can be facilitated by granting a short sale, or by accepting a deed in lieu of foreclosure. Some may be more than eager to hand you the keys and deed to the property in exchange for being let off the hook for the debt. In many cases that may be a great win for all sides.

If they would like to stay and keep their property while avoiding foreclosure then there are a number of options for modifying the loan note to make that happen. These include recapitalization of past due amounts, principal reductions, adjusting the rate or term, escalating payments, and any combination of these.

For example: maybe a borrower fell behind on payments because of a temporary job loss due to a personal injury. Maybe they just couldn't catch up, and their previous noteholder wouldn't work with them. Now they may have been back at work for a few years, and are keeping on top of their other bills. By adding their past due amount back to the balance of the loan, and extending payments for a few years, they may be able to just start making their payments again. If you like you can sweeten the deal and relationship by steadily increasing payments back up to their normal amount over time.

Dealing with Defaulters

What if the borrower re-defaults on this agreement, or just refuses to work with you, or make any attempt to help themselves? It can happen. In my personal experience this has only been in around 5% of cases, out of millions of dollars in loans. If they just can't afford the property, and they really aren't ready for homeownership then they may need to be foreclosed on. You can process the foreclosure yourself, bring in an attorney, or sell the note to someone that wants the property. There are lots of investors looking to use notes to take down great investment properties.

Going Above & Beyond

If you are someone that enjoys going above and beyond to help others, and who thrives on creative problem solving there are plenty of opportunities to do that here. I love it. It keeps investing personally rewarding and interesting.
I really enjoy this side of note investing. There are

borrowers that are really great people, which can translate into really great borrowers, all they need is a little extra help. Some need help beefing up their income. Others need some money management skills. They don't teach you how to budget or manage a mortgage in school, and that's a terrible thing. It leaves virtually every student underserved and ill prepared when they graduate. This might work out okay for creditors and a system that preys on these individuals in the short term, but it hurts the individual, their families, and everyone else in the long run.

We've certainly gone the extra mile in our organization. We've helped people find jobs so that they can get back on track and save their homes, we've connected people to assistance so that can make ends meet and keep the heat on, and we've even provided counseling on how to minimize their monthly bills so that they can create the financial surplus they need to make their mortgage payments on time and enjoy a better life. It's completely game changing for them.

Six creative ideas for helping struggling borrowers:

1. Get them a job with one of your vendors or partners
2. Connect them to local assistance to catch up on utility

bills
3. Refer them to local finance and grant programs for making energy efficient improvements
4. Help them negotiate away other debt and payments
5. Refer them to financial counseling services
6. Offer escalating payment plans

Customer Service

Customer service is a very important part of a note business. Big banks and mortgage lenders are terrible at customer service. There may be one or two exceptions, and they do very well. But in general big institutions either don't see great customer service as valuable, or they are incapable of delivering it. Don't underestimate the value and importance of good service.

Consumers are increasingly putting an emphasis on service, and they are voting for those that can deliver it with their wallets. This will continue to separate those that are successful, or not, as well as the level of that success.

If you are going to operate an actual note business or fund this is critical. Strive to provide great service to your borrowers, capital partners, and your vendors. Good service will go a long way to enhancing the performance, returns on, and value of your notes and business. It increases borrower loyalty, and borrowers will go the extra mile to make their payments on time. Treating capital partners well will encourage them to keep investing with you, and to refer others. Good service to vendors means they'll enjoy working with you, will go the extra mile when you need it, and may even give you better deals.

Not sure how to excel in this area? Think about some of the terrible and excellent customer experiences you've had lately. Have you been driven almost mad by mobile phone companies or cable providers that can't answer the phone, show up on time, or deliver accurate bills? Has your bank nickel and dimed you with junk fees, made a profit off of you by delaying your funds, or made it difficult to get your own money? What about the good experiences? Maybe it was just a friendly smile and an eager to help attitude. Maybe a simple customer service rep that actually strived to help you fix an issue. Perhaps it was simply getting to speak to a live person!

So think about all the things that have turned you off to other businesses, and eradicate them from yours. Think about the times you've been wowed by great experiences – incorporate more of those, as standard. Empower your team members to actually help, and have an accessible service team.

Turning Distress Into Success

Chapter 11:

Reducing Risk

How do you minimize risk in note investing and operating a note business or fund?

You can't only focus on the upside with unquenchable optimism. Maximizing returns over time is equally about squashing risks. For me note investing stands out as a great choice thanks to the mechanics of notes as an asset, the many exit strategies available, the low volatility, and the safety compared to direct investment in bricks and mortar. But if I were tell you that there was "zero" risk that wouldn't be completely accurate either. There is risk in every single type of investment out there. There is risk in even keeping your money in a bank savings account, CD, or in cash under your mattress or in a safe in your closet. There is risk in trying to get a job and work for 'the man' for the rest of your life and hoping for social security to provide for your retirement. Personally I am drawn to notes as much for their safety as their upside. So how do we go beyond that and drive risks down, as close to zero as we possibly can?

There are actually many ways to eliminate, account for, and insulate against risk, including:

- Reducing risk in your organization
- Reducing investment risks
- Recognizing specific threats to notes
- Insulating your overall finances
- Increasing our knowledge and skills
- Getting expert advice

Mitigating Management

Those choosing to invest in notes at scale, or to start a note brokerage, business, or fund also need to account for their size, operational, and management risk. With the extra pros of more volume and money, come extra risks or factors to watch. This includes simply ensuring the wheels keep turning, ensuring compliance, and being mindful that so many others rely on performance.

Smart mitigation of risk in this area includes:

- Solid business planning
- Detailed record keeping and organization
- Maintaining liquidity and reserves
- Insurance (business, income, and key person insurance)
- Adherence to sound business principles and ethics
- Having failsafe measures in place, in advance

When it comes to running a business, especially if you are active in it, one of the biggest risks is if you, or another key employee can't show up. What happens then? Will things keep working? Systems and automation can help ensure income keeps coming in, and returns go to those they are supposed to, and employees keep getting paid. But there is still often a human element. What if you have to take a couple weeks off for a family emergency? Do you have someone training as a general manager who can step up and fill the void? Is there a system or manual that they can turn to in order to keep everything moving without having to text or call you every five minutes? Do you have backups screened or training for other roles? Do you have key person insurance just in case someone is out of action for an extended period of time, or something happens to them that prevents them from returning to work?

Compliance is a big challenge in this arena too. Banking, lending, and finance regulation is always changing. You've got to be proactive about staying on top of these changes. This also means it can pay to have legal counsel you can go to for help to navigate changes and stay in compliance. Outsourcing certain parts of the business help to mitigate compliance risk and streamline management too. For example, collections. If you are taking on unsecured debt, or have to go to the foreclosure stage, it can be better to delegate that to a pro who is licensed.

Reducing Risk in Investing

There are five pillars of reducing risk in investing:

1. Learning and knowledge
2. Due diligence
3. Being alert to, and preventing specific threats to an investment
4. Defenses for preserving wealth and income
5. Diversification

Until now there has been very little real education available on note investing. There have been occasional seminars by those selling notes, and some really complex and dense books on the financial system, but that isn't really effective or helpful for the average person that wants to invest in notes intelligently and safely. That's why we created the National Note Academy, and now this book.

What are some of the other, specific risks to note investments after a note has been acquired? And what are some of the tools to minimize and protect against them?

Fuquan Bilal

Borrower Habits & Lifestyle

An individual borrower's habits and lifestyle can impact the value and performance of a note. A good healthy borrower that does things right can be an incredible asset, and can increase the value of the collateral and note. You might go even further in helping these borrowers. Then there may be the rare case where a borrower is found to be running an illegal grow operation, turning the property into a meth lab, or who is into other bad habits. That can put a property at risk. What you can do as a noteholder may be more limited than as a landlord, but you can act accordingly. You might move more quickly to foreclosure, offer more incentives for them to refinance or sell, or otherwise dispose of the note, without lumbering unexpected risk on someone else. In severe cases clauses in the paperwork may allow you to accelerate the note.

Property Taxes

Non-payment of property taxes can jeopardize a note. Over a period of years delinquent property taxes can lead to foreclosure and auction. In buoyant times, when equity is high this can actually be a good thing, at least when you get paid early. Yet, this is why lenders often demand property taxes are escrowed each month. This way the lender and noteholder has control over the situation.

HOA & Condo Dues

Homeowner association and condo dues are much like property taxes. They can become a lien against a property and lead to foreclosure too. Some note investors really dislike loans on these properties for this reason. Others prefer them because associations can help keep up property value, protect building exteriors, and often they can be in very affluent areas. In any case, dues are a factor to watch and keep on top of.

Property Condition & Maintenance

While the underlying land is often responsible for the bulk of value and appreciation in compared to brick and mortar improvements, serious blows to property condition can be a pain. This is especially true in the case of hurricanes. Insurance, and even various insurances are used to protect against this. The lender and noteholder is normally protected by mandatory insurance requirements in the paperwork, as well as having co-signing authority for the release of insurance funds.

Wealth Preservation

Whether you are investing in notes or not, or are investing completely passively in a small way, or are on your way to building an international financial empire it is critical to think about asset protection, wealth preservation, and insulation from risk. The earlier you start to incorporate these measures the better protected you will be, and the less any costs will be. In fact, if you wait, you may actually undo any potential protections some of these strategies offer.

Some of the tools to assist in this include:

- Trusts and corporate entities
- Reinsurance
- Self-directed IRAs
- Protecting your personal information
- Advanced encryption for communications
- A good attorney on retainer

All of these items will help provide a cushion and buffer from liability. They can also decrease your appeal as a victim. There are plenty of fraudsters out there. There are auto insurance fraud rings, opportunistic borrowers, and bad attorneys that fuel their unscrupulous greed. Unfortunately, not everyone will be happy as you grow more successful and wealthier. It can breed jealousy, and make you a target. It's sad but true. But there is a lot you can do to minimize your appeal as a victim. If you have your home address and phone number on everything publicly, have multi-million dollar houses in your name, and flash a lot of cash, someone is going to want a piece of that. If you look like an easy target it isn't difficult for someone to pull you into a malicious or frivolous lawsuit, or even try to blackmail you in some way. This is true for anyone that starts making progress in wealth building, from any source. Now if you have good layers of protection it will be too expensive and taxing for most to try and take advantage of you and get anywhere. This can also add a lot of protection in case you are ever in a major accident, go bankrupt, or are involved in a divorce, or someone in your family is. Keeping business and investment finances separate provides a great barrier. If your business is ever in trouble it will be less likely you'll have any personal liability. And if you run into personal problems, the chances that your business and investment assets and income will survive are much better.

Diversification

Diversification is the foundation of all wealth preservation and sustainable wealth building. Whether you are starting out with $5k or $5B you don't want to lose your principal. You can do your best to make wise investments, but you can't ever 110% control the future all the time. This makes diversification key. Even going back to the days of King Solomon, who was regarded as one of the wealthiest and wisest people of all time, he recommended diversifying seven or eight ways. For most reading about investing in notes is a form of diversification itself. How much you'll invest in notes really depends on where you are at financially. Some may need to plow the bulk of what they have into notes to get a head start, before diversifying into other asset classes and strategies. Others may need to put a large percentage of their investment portfolio into notes to account for slow growth, or high risk elsewhere in their portfolio. Some may wish to just allocate a sound 30% in notes for the long term.

However, where notes can really reveal one of their best advantages is in the double or triple layers of diversification they offer; such as when investing in a note fund or multiple notes at the same time. Out of 3 notes one may underperform expectations, but one will probably be on target, and the third may do far better than expected. Then as we already covered there are many different types of notes. You may invest in first mortgages, second mortgages, auto loans, and credit card debt. This can all be spread around the country and at different price points and credit levels. Then when investing in multifamily properties, or office or retail property notes there is even more diversification. In a note on a multifamily apartment building there may be 100 or 300 two income households contributing to the performance of that note. Not everyone will do great all the time, but not everyone will be doing poorly at the same time either. Then there is retail. In a boutique strip mall you may have a Walmart or grocery store which thrives in good and bad times, discount dollar stores, and high end boutique clothing or jewelry stores, and restaurants. In good or bad times some of these retailers are always likely to be thriving.

Expert Help

We've already talked about building a team and putting together a board of advisors, but it can't be repeated enough. Don't just delegate down, hire up, and get the best and most experienced people on your team that you can. Hire people smarter than you, more experienced than you, and if possible; that even care more than you. Get a mastermind group of mentors together that can give you a second opinion on our plans, help you avoid the pitfalls, and propel your success. Find pros you can lean on for advice, coaches, mentors, and even peers that can act as accountability partners. They can all help you preserve your wealth, and make the most of what you've got.

Turning Distress Into Success

Chapter 12:

Stress Free Success

We've covered a lot of the nuts and bolts and circuitry of note investing safely, profitably, and at a higher level. But it really doesn't have to be that complicated. And investing and building incredible income and wealth doesn't have to be a grind, or boring, or cramp life now. In fact, maximizing both note investing, and life, is intricately intertwined. So how can we enjoy more stress free success?

Stress free success doesn't come automatically. In fact rushing to make a lot of money often turns into a lot of stress, and sometimes that ultimately sabotages future success. But enhancing your finances and reaching your monetary goals doesn't have to derail the rest of your life, and it shouldn't. And wanting to enjoy more of the free things in life doesn't have to, and shouldn't mean sacrificing financial success, so that you can have more of that for longer, and on a greater scale. But true success in all areas of life, and even just successfully investing in notes without pulling your hair out isn't going to happen without some thought, and a plan.

Planning for Success

How do you plan for success, and stress free success, so that you grow richer in every area of life?

At the beginning of this book we looked at specific financial goals and timelines. This is a crucial pillar of achieving what we want. But it isn't the only element in a solid plan. You can't have a great, complete financial plan, work schedule, or business plan unless you identify what you don't want too, and schedule in the other things that you do want. No one plans to fall into distress, but if you don't plan for success, that's what you get.

So wherever you are going make sure you plan, and schedule in what you want in all areas of life. Don't put off your core goals and focus until you've hit some really big future financial goal. Keep what matters most in focus, and make time for it.

Then you can break that out into annual planning, monthly goals, and create daily actions and habits that deliver on it all.

Decide to Enjoy the Ride

Not everything will go as planned. Planning helps, but it isn't bulletproof, and plans change. But we can decide to enjoy the ride no matter what. When you invest in notes you'll have amazing days when the stars align and things are better than you ever dreamed possible. Then there can be days as a business owner when one of your team members really drops the ball, or jumps ship. If we pay attention there are magical, priceless moments every day. Then there are those we'd love for the Men in Black to show up and permanently delete from our memories. We can influence a lot, but we can't control everything all the time. The only exception is our perspective and our own actions. Decide now to enjoy the ride, no matter what ups, downs, and twists are on the rollercoaster track between here and the finish line.

Operating at 100%

To get more of what we want on the ride, and to achieve the maximum amount of success, we've got to operate at 100%.

If we want 100% out, we've got to put 100% in. No this doesn't mean putting all of your money into notes, or 100% of your time and energy. It's about operating at 100% of your potential in every area, all the time.

This means operating at 100% in terms of health, mental capacity, in the right actions, in the right direction, at your full potential in that moment. Prior to reading this book some might have been at their full potential doing half a push up, working a grueling 9-5 and a 6 to 12, and maybe having the bandwidth to drop a few coins in someone's hat, or helping an old lady across the road. Investing in notes could mean soon having the ability to work four hours a week, to help others with tens of thousands of dollars, and even save their homes, or just to spend more time keeping in shape.

Real estate columnist and business consultant Tim Houghten has a great example of this leap. He explains that after quitting school and going to work in the foodservice industry, one manager told him that if he wanted a raise he should start performing the tasks of the next level manager and prove his worth first. At the time that seemed like a conundrum. At the time, like most workers his mentality was *"I'm not getting paid what I'm worth; pay me more, and then I'll do more."* After learning about real estate, and being given $500 to get his mortgage license by his father-in-law, Tim made $127,000 the first month he opened his mortgage business. It didn't take long to hit the million dollar a year mark, and to make as much as $60,000 in one hour.

For me, operating at 100% not only means being in the mortgage note business, but being at the top of my game in personal operational capacity. For me that means eating healthy, keeping in shape, continuous learning, getting enough sleep, etc. When I'm at my best, in my optimal zone, I'm operating at my 100% potential.

Building Good Habits

Getting to operating at 100%, reaching maximum potential, and enjoying a smooth process is all about good habits. It doesn't happen overnight. Especially not if it is to be sustainable. It's about consistent steps in the right direction – developing good habits.

This is really about replicating success. What are those

that are living the life you want doing? What habits have helped them get to where they are, and stay on top? One of my personal favorites is meditation. But don't be afraid to put your own twist on things. May be eating a better, more balanced diet, practicing yoga every morning, reading daily, and ritually contributing a set amount of your paycheck to investing in notes each month is the right move for you. These types of good habits are the foundation of a more successful lifestyle, which is sustainable.

Automation & Systemization

Maybe you feel you are already doing incredible in the good habits department. Congratulations. I personally, like to strive for constant improvement; always finding ways to challenge myself and find incremental growth. These concepts directly relate to note investing and businesses as well. They apply to making investments, building wealth, and how you operate your business and treat your team. It's just in business we refer to this as automation and systems. So how can we get our investments, finances, and life all aligned and synched together?

For those just starting out look for ways to systemize and automate savings. Do it by using automatic transfers to savings based on card spending or automatic transfers right when you get paid. Then commit to setting aside a certain amount each month, quarter, or year to invest in notes. There are even smartphone apps like Entrust's which can help you do this through a self-directed IRA. For professionals that already have good incomes invest what you can now, and commit to investing a percentage of your salary each year into what is working for you.

In terms of operating a note business; the more you automate and systemize the more effortless and stress free it will be. Virtually all marketing from blogs to Google Ads, to direct mail and email marketing can be automated today. Aweber and WordPress and some good tools to help you get started here. Then internally if you document the process and create a system for everything you do the first time, then someone else can pick up the task and run with it. This applies to everything from sourcing notes, to bidding on pools of mortgage notes, to dealing with borrower issues, reselling notes, and even distributing returns to anyone that has invested money with you. That means more time freedom for you, confidence in a system that can work while you sleep, and that new team members can be plugged in as needed, while maintaining a seamless experience for everyone you deal with.

Life Balance

We can't end this chapter without really touching on life balance, and specifically personal and family relationships. You really can't wait until you are generating six or seven figures from notes to spend time with your family, kids, or significant other. No matter how short of a period that is, you'll be losing priceless time that you'll never be able to get back. If you make enough money you might be able to extend your life a little, but you can't get lost time back. So how can you add note investing to what you are doing, and without starving your relationships of even more time?

This may not be an issue for everyone. Perhaps you are already retired and just need the income and higher returns from notes. But others may still be juggling a promising career, hectic business, or several jobs just to make ends meet and keep up with the Joneses. Choosing a streamlined totally passive method of investing in notes doesn't have to take up more than a couple hours a year. Just set a time each year to review and recalibrate your portfolio.

However, even those looking to build note businesses can find ways to create better balance. This isn't going to happen magically, unless you schedule it in. Literally schedule in time for personal activities, and block them out. If you don't, work is going to creep in and take over. Many of the factors, tactics, and actions we've covered in this book are also perfect for crossing over. Some great examples of this include; taking your spouse with you to industry conferences or out to dinners, dedicating individual notes to your kids and tracking their performance with them, or bringing your teens in as interns during the summer. This is incredible bonding time, full of memorable moments, and great teaching times.

You Can Do This!

You can invest in notes, and win. We've covered a lot about different types of notes, how to complete due diligence and even create your own fund, but note investing doesn't have to be that complex. Whether you want to begin investing one note at a time, or to build a billion-dollar mortgage note business, there are many ways to simplify, streamline, and align your whole life goals so that you can enjoy for of what you want now, while working on the bigger financial milestones. If you want the higher returns, income and security, note investing offers an option that will fit your lifestyle. You can do it.

What's Next...

Thanks for reading. Years of learning and testing went into this book. Now you know what compelled me to begin investing in notes, and why I do it the way I do. We've really covered most of the A-Z of investing in notes. You've learned how the banks and wealthiest individuals on the planet use notes to preserve and increase their wealth and incomes. We've discovered the leap from what the average person does to try to improve their finances, and how the leap to notes can make a massive difference and give individual investors an advantage. You've discovered the power of the paper, its safety mechanisms and multiple exit strategies, and even how to minimize risk and triple protect your investment performance with the deep diversification note investing can offer. You've been introduced to a wide range of investment options and strategies so that you can take your own finances from distress to success, or from good to great, sustainably. Now you even have the insight on how you can raise substantial capital to scale your investments or launch your own fund, how to power negotiate, and run a note business efficiently and profitably. We've even dug into how to enjoy amazing life balance while you enhance your finances through notes. So how can you get started investing in notes right away and begin enjoying more?

Why YOU Need to Invest in Notes

Note investing isn't just for everyone that wants higher returns on their investments, who wants passive income cash flow, or wants to build wealth and improve wealth preservation. It offers all of these things, and often does a much better job than the alternatives. But you aren't going to begin benefiting from all of this unless you take action. You've got to put what you've learned in this book into play. And there is no time like the present.

But it's more than just about better returns. If that's all you are after, invest in a note today. There is so much more though. The nation needs more lienlords like you. People need *you*. Borrowers, homeowners, business owners, communities, and other individual investors need more people like you to be noteholders and conduits for better lending. And this could well be the pinnacle of your potential. The zone in which you are truly operating at 100% in life, and which can facilitate all of your other goals from wealth building to family to philanthropy.

I want this for you. I invested many hours and dollars in putting this book together and getting it in front of you so that you can share in the rewards that I am experiencing in my life. It's not just the really big things either. For example, I could never imagine having to be stuck in horrible traffic commuting back and forth to a miserable job day after day again. When I do venture out around rush hour today my jaw drops in bewilderment at how people put up with that, and subject themselves to that. You don't have to waste hours of your life each week on that hamster wheel. And even if you are a highly paid professional or CEO this still probably includes you too. I don't want you to give up anything you are passionate about. Run that organization, save people's lives as a doctor, or whatever you care about. But enjoy doing it because you can and with the freedom to operate at 100% while knowing your finances are taken care of.

At some scale *you need* notes working for you. The sector and individuals could really use someone like you involved too. So *don't hesitate.*

Act Now

I've given you as much information as I could pack into this book. The facts and advantages of investing in notes really speak for themselves. But I can't do everything for you. You still have to take action. There is no time like the present. I don't mind if you invest in one of the methods I've mentioned, or you carve your own path, I just want you to keep moving to get more of want you want, need, and should have.

The truth is that there are only so many tomorrows. So wade in. Grab a note if you can and add it to your portfolio. If you want to learn more I'll provide some resources in a moment. But get started and learn and earn at the same time. If you want to start your own note business or fund, open up Google and make some appointments with the pros you need in your corner to make it happen.

This is an incredible time to invest in notes. The sooner you start the better. Get into notes and start protecting what you've got better right now. Start investing in notes today and begin enjoying the compound, and potentially tax free advantages so that you begin snowballing the good results.

Get Started Right Here

1. Learn more about notes
2. Buy notes online via the NNG Trade Desk

Learn More About Notes

The NNG Note Academy offers even more information on investing in notes and a virtual resource center for continuously growing note investing knowledge. This incorporates articles, FAQs, webinars, videos, and coaching calls. You'll even find higher learning courses on investing in second mortgages and practice note opportunities. Get all the up to the minute tips and news by following @infonng on Twitter.

Don't forget to share! Everyone you know deserves the chance to learn about note investing. Share the links with them online, on your favorite social media networks, or gift them a copy of this book.

I'd love to hear from you too. Let me know how your journey unfolds; your success, questions, winning moves, and how it helps enhance your life and how you've been able to help others...

To your success!
Fuquan Bilal

<u>www.nngnoteacademy.com</u>
<u>www.nationalnotegroup.com</u>

ENDNOTES

CHAPTER 3

[1]
http://www.federalreserve.gov/econresdata/releases/morto
utstand/current.htm

CHAPTER 4

[1] http://www.realtytrac.com/news/realtytrac-reports/q1-
2015-u-s-residential-loan-origination-report/
[2] https://www.nerdwallet.com/blog/credit-card-
data/average-credit-card-debt-household/
[3] https://www.mba.org/2015-press-releases/mortgage-
bankers%E2%80%99-commercial/multifamily-originations-
rise-to-400-billion-in-2014
[4]
http://www.nationalmortgagenews.com/news/servicing/red
efaults-continue-to-plague-hamp-1045414-1.html

CHAPTER 5

[1] http://money.cnn.com/2015/04/21/retirement/retirement-
confidence/